PRAISE FOR *ROOTS OF RESILIENCE*

One of the greatest joys of someone who teaches others is to watch those they guide mature into the person they had the potential to become. Having known and worked with Emily for over a decade as an advisor, teacher, colleague, and friend, it is such a joy and blessing to see how she has combined her family's story, professional journey, and collective life experiences to realize her many aspirations.

Her book, *Roots of Resilience*, is not only a testament to her remarkable journey but also an homage to the many essential attributes that one needs to successfully navigate life. It is a wonderfully crafted and heartfelt message that will surely resonate with the reader, regardless of who you are or where you come from.

Emily's story is a message of gratitude to those whose sacrifices and unwavering principles have inspired the lives of others, empowering them to positively influence their communities. It is a message of clarity to those of us venturing through life, for sometimes it is not until we have traveled down the path and stopped for a moment of reflection that we realize the true impact of our decisions, the invaluable magnitude of those who crossed our path, and the miraculous transformation that has occurred along the way. And it is a message of guidance for those yet to begin their journey. By highlighting the power of courage, resilience, motivation, and faith that it takes to seize opportunity and achieve remarkable feats, *Roots of Resilience* serves as a beacon of hope, inspiration, and a steady compass that can guide us all through the trials of this challenging and uncertain life.

—Kelton T. Stewart, DDS, MS
Chair, Department of Orthodontics and Oral Facial Genetics, Indiana University School of Dentistry

During the Vietnam War, I was one of two women who approached the pastor of the First Mennonite Church in Berne, Indiana, seeking support to help resettle a refugee family. After a period of anxious waiting, we were blessed to welcome the Taing family into our community.

This moving book, written by Dr. Emily Taing Watson—a daughter of the young couple who escaped Cambodia—recounts the harrowing journey her extended family endured as they fled the Khmer Rouge regime, survived a refugee camp in Thailand, and eventually built a new life in the United States. Through her storytelling, we witness the family's incredible resilience, strength, and determination.

Inspired by her family's perseverance, Dr. Watson pursued a successful career as an orthodontist. I am proud to say that my friendship with the Taing family has remained strong for over forty-five years, and it has been an honor to witness their journey firsthand.

—Marge Habegger

Emily Watson's story stopped me in my tracks.

Decades ago, her grandfather dared to dream—fleeing war-torn Cambodia with a hope for something better. Not for himself, but for the generations that would come after him. His son, Emily's father, would carry that dream forward, waking up before the sun to run a donut shop, day after day, year after year. And now, Emily—his daughter and that grandfather's legacy—is one of the most successful orthodontists in her entire county.

That's not just a story about success. That's a story about resilience. About sacrifice. About the kind of hard work that doesn't always make headlines but changes lives. It's about the faithfulness of God through every step, every struggle, every unseen prayer.

One generation's courage can open doors for the next. And Emily is living proof.

What a powerful reminder that no dream is wasted when it's sown in faith and watered with grit. This is legacy. This is hope. This is the kind of story that reminds us why we keep believing for more—not just for ourselves, but for those coming behind us.

—Kondo Simfuke

Pastor, advocate, and national speaker

In this deeply moving and inspiring memoir, Dr. Emily Taing Watson takes us on a journey of resilience, sacrifice, and triumph. The daughter of parents who escaped the horrors of the Khmer Rouge regime in Cambodia, she shares the incredible story of how they built a new life from the ground up in the United States. Their unwavering determination, work ethic, and love for family form the foundation of Emily's own success. Through their example, she learned the true meaning of perseverance and the power of following one's dreams.

As an orthodontist, Emily not only built a thriving private practice but also cultivated a work environment where her team can flourish, learn, and grow. Her vision to create a Strengths-Based Practice is nothing short of transformative. In her office, every person is empowered to discover their talents and leverage them for success. The compassion she shows her patients and team is only matched by her drive to help others reach their full potential. Her story is a testament to the power of resilience, the importance of family, and the incredible impact one person can have on the lives of many.

For anyone seeking inspiration, guidance, or simply a reminder of the strength of the human spirit, this book is a must-read. It is a true celebration of courage, leadership, and the unwavering belief in the possibility of a better future.

—Vicki Newell

Coach and consultant, Gallup Strength

ROOTS *of* RESILIENCE

ROOTS *of* RESILIENCE

LESSONS IN COURAGE, FAMILY,
AND THE POWER OF SHOWING UP EVERY DAY

Dr. Emily Taing Watson

Advantage | Books

Published by Advantage Books, Charleston, South Carolina.
An imprint of Advantage Media.

Printed in the United States of America.

10 9 8 7 6 5 4 3 2 1

ISBN: 979-8-89188-125-9 (Paperback)
ISBN: 979-8-89188-126-6 (eBook)

Library of Congress Control Number: 2025908627

Cover design by Matthew Morse.
Layout design by Ruthie Wood.

07-14-2025 1:48

To my parents, Ty and Ky Taing. May this book honor you for your courage, hard work, love, and endless sacrifice you've shown throughout my life.

CONTENTS

ptember 9, 1980 Vol. 3 No. 19

aing Relatives Arrive

iting, crying, and sharing continued
o the early morning hours.
The eleven new Chinese Cambodian
ugees are living in the former Post-
d house, next to the Taing family.
extend them a warm welcome to the
rch and community.

By SHARON LITTLE
and BECKY RICHARDS

Beginning today, the halls and classrooms of Central Catholic High School, closed for school purposes since 1972, will ring again with life — this time with the voices of Indochinese refugees.

Through the efforts of Bishop William McManus, the Diocese of Fort Wayne-South Bend, and Catholic Charities, Vietnamese, Cambodian, Laotian and Hmong refugees will be temporarily housed, dormitory style, in the now largely unused building at South Clinton and Lewis streets. The Hmong are hill tribesmen in Laos.

Erik Henry, refugee coordinator for Catholic Charities, which began the Indochinese resettlement program four years ago, said eight refugees will be staying at the school beginning tonight and "we are hoping within three weeks to have the total resettlement program (including offices and four staff members) operating out of Central Catholic."

Henry and John Martin, charities director, said in-

Free at last!

Taing relatives begi

INTRODUCTION

The past lives within the present, and our ancestors breathe through our children.

~ ELIF SHAFAK

We each play many roles. I am an orthodontist, a businesswoman, a practice owner and employer, a wife, a mother, a daughter, a sister, a member of a church, and part of the fabric of the communities where I practice; my role changes, but who I am at my core does not. And I believe that essential, unwavering core and strength stem from the example of my parents. They are Cambodian refugees of Chinese descent who escaped the horrors, crimes against humanity, and genocide of Pol Pot, eventually making their way to the United States with nothing more than the clothes on their backs, and who, through hard work and sacrifice, created a family, started a successful small business, and, through determination and faith, built our beautiful lives here.

As a first-generation child of immigrants, I always innately understood that my life was a little different from my friends' lives. My parents were loving and kind but much stricter than the parents of kids around me. In fact, I have been asked to speak to groups of students, some of whom are first generation, to tell them that, yes, you can be from a "different" family, perhaps one in which your parents don't speak English well or you have customs from another country—but you can take the best of that world, its traditions, and your own ambitions and be successful here.

In my family, there was a strong emphasis on education—and being sure I got all A's. My parents, when they were young, had to stop going to school because of the danger of bombs. Consequently, they encouraged me to really value the free education and learning I was obtaining in the United States. They could not understand *not* appreciating that opportunity. My father would tell me that only in the United States could you go to school for free—or even be paid to go to school with scholarships.

Part of their push to have my siblings and me study hard was the difficult path they had to take as small business owners. My parents never took a day off—they worked multiple jobs, saving to buy their first donut shop, which my father kept open even on Christmas morning. We never took a vacation. I saw firsthand that hard work is honorable and essential to success—but not always convenient, pretty, or fun.

My school friends—and no doubt many people reading this—have or had parents who told them to finish their supper because around the world, there are those who go hungry. And in my home as a child, we wasted not one grain of rice. My mother hated—and still hates—throwing any food in the trash. The lesson my mother taught us was the story of the great swaths of starvation throughout Cambodia during the terrorizing reign of the Khmer Rouge, in which between 1.5 and 2 million people died—including some members of our family who were not fortunate enough to escape.

However, what is so important to my life, and to this book, is that my parents never displayed bitterness—despite it being completely understandable if they had felt that way. Instead, they imbued me with gratitude. For example, instead of complaining about the long hours they worked, often with just a few hours of sleep, they considered themselves blessed to be in the United States and blessed to have children who were allowed an education and the freedoms here. In my parents' minds, we embodied the American dream.

Now, as a grown woman with a thriving orthodontic practice, a happy family of my own, and a life beyond my parents' dreams when they arrived, I see they were right. I am living that hope, living that dream. Ultimately, I know they survived in order for their family to thrive here. This knowledge has instilled in me a deep sense of gratitude.

Though I went to school for years in order to graduate with a degree in my specialty, when I set out to write this book, I realized that I learned many, if not most, of my core business and life lessons from the example of my parents. I also realized that these lessons are timeless ones of courage, gratitude, hard work, and overcoming obstacles—lessons for everyone. They are leadership lessons, and I use them every day in my own way.

When I was in dental school, I did not yet realize that factors such as leadership and success principles and types of leadership were important—especially if you elect to take the more difficult pathway of purchasing and owning a practice. However, one day, while I was still in my residency, I had a foreshadowing that I needed to hone my people-management skills. Someone in an assisting program was assigned to do x-rays with me. I was in a time crunch, and in my haste to finish, I was abrupt with that person, leaving her with hurt feelings. Afterward, a faculty member discussed the situation with me. "I understand you were in a rush and needed to get this done," he said, "but six months from now, you are going to graduate and will have an entire group of people you need to lead."

That was my initial wake-up call. Leadership was a new concept to me, even though I had worked hard to achieve my dream of becoming an orthodontist—one of the most competitive areas of dentistry. Leading *people* was something else entirely.

I started studying leadership development by listening to audiobooks, one of which happened to be *StrengthsFinder 2.0*, which is based on a study by the Gallup organization and advocates focusing on strengths rather than weaknesses. So, before I purchased my practice, I already had at least an inkling that running operations required knowledge of more than just orthodontics. My biggest challenges would be supervising, developing, and coaching my team. Clearly, though, I hadn't realized to what degree I would need to focus on how I wanted to lead my employees.

But as I thought of my own strengths—and weaknesses—I could not help but see that it was my parents' influence that gave me a drive to succeed and pushed me to where I am now. They showed me how to treat employees and family—how to have a workplace where people feel cared for. They showed me that hard work is the only pathway to the top. We each must overcome adversity in life. It is my sincere hope that the adversities you face are not those of people such as my parents, fleeing unthinkable hardship. However, within each of us is that survival gene, that fierceness and tenacity we can hopefully call up from somewhere that will give us the grit to succeed. *That* is the strength we need to draw from.

It is my hope that the story of my family and the lessons I learned can inspire you. Sometimes, our greatest leadership lessons are found in the people closest to us and in our ancestors.

ptember 9, 1980 Vol. 3 No. 19
aing Relatives Arrive
Free at last!
Taing relatives begi

CHAPTER 1

It Starts with Courage

Your struggles are someone else's blessings.

~ KY TAING, MY MOTHER

I know people who wear their late grandmother's ring or their father's watch, almost like a talisman, for luck or courage. But my parents escaped the Khmer Rouge in Cambodia with just the clothing on their backs. My inheritance is their character, which is as much a part of me as breathing. One of the most important traits I have observed in them and hope I also embody is courage—to me, courage is the bedrock of all the other lessons my parents taught me.

But, like every person, I have those days when I am filled with doubt.

None more so than the day I decided to purchase my practice. I had, like most doctors and dentists in this country, graduated with massive student loan debt in the hundreds of thousands of dollars. Now I would be taking on additional debt to buy the practice—which also had two locations. These numbers were overwhelming to me and filled me with a bit of panic (maybe more than a bit).

But, as with nearly every big decision or moment, when I needed the voice of someone wise, someone else's counsel, I turned to my parents.

My mother said, "I know that is a lot of money, Emily."

Believe me, I knew. "It's crazy of me to even consider this, isn't it? Do you think it's going to be OK?"

At the time—and still true today—most new graduates in my field preferred to join large existing practices rather than purchasing a practice. That way, they can earn a secure salary while not having to deal with the human resources side of things and the practicalities of running a practice. Yet here I was, about to sign papers to do the opposite.

But my parents were so calm, reminding me that I was investing in *myself.* My mother actually said that this big loan was not like buying a car, where once you drive the car off the lot, it depreciates. This was investing in something far more powerful. In *me.* In my future. In the future of the family I hoped to one day start with my husband. Rather than working for someone else, as my parents had when they had first arrived in the United States, putting in long hours on their way to becoming small business owners, my father assured me that I was worth believing in and that I could do it.

My entire life, actually, they have told me I could do what I put my mind to.

However, there was a wrinkle. A rather big but wonderful wrinkle. As I was preparing to purchase the practice, my husband and I made the decision that it was not the best time to start a family. I was taking on so much after completing an intensive residency, and now I would be the owner of a practice and have to learn to navigate that—everything from managing staff to ensuring the office was clean to learning all about my patients. And then, the week before I signed the papers to buy the practice, I found out I was pregnant.

As wonderful as that blessing was, I was soon working—and throwing up all day in between seeing patients. I was exhausted and stressed, and because the practice I bought had two locations, I was driving an hour or more each way every day of the week. This was not the start to my practice that I had envisioned.

However, throughout my life, I have always had a different view on "tough stuff." Courage can only exist if there are fear and difficulties—otherwise, you would not need courage.

On my worst days, I think of what my parents had to do to survive. It feels like a miracle that they were able to escape the brutality of their home country. While still in Cambodia, my mother once got so ill from malaria that she thought she was going to die—they didn't have any medication—and this was not the only illness she faced. My parents literally survived Cambodia for the opportunity to come to a country they could not possibly even have imagined while growing up in their small village. I am the product of their deep courage—and to see what they have accomplished in one generation is an incredible story of perseverance, tenacity, and all of the traits we will explore in this book.

My parents' courage was demonstrated not only by their escape to the United States—but also by the fact that they left family behind and all they ever knew. My mother left her own family and came to the United States with my father's immediate family. She was only twenty and did not see her mother from 1979 until 1991. I am very close to my parents and can barely comprehend the loneliness and the pain of such a monumental decision. I think very few people born in the United States can understand what it must take to leave everything, including your language, your culture, the beauty of your country and what you treasure about it, your precious mementos, and the people and clan you love, and come here and make your way.

To be honest, even the act of marriage for my parents was a testament to their courage. They barely knew each other—but the regime was splitting up families. If my mother had revealed that she was a single woman of twenty at the time, living with her mom, she would have been sent away or forced to marry someone the regime chose for her. She told me that they would likely have forced her into a marriage with someone who had disabilities caused by a landmine, had been injured by the war, or was otherwise unable to care for her in any way. The same would have happened to my father. Marrying each other was the wiser choice.

In fact, my mother's mother had turned down two men who had asked to marry my mother—once, when my mother was thirteen, and then again at fifteen. My grandmother had said that my mother was just a girl. But this time with my dad, as a young adult, she would be safer being married. It would be better for both of my parents. It was an arranged marriage, one forced by the suffering of war. I know that I was so excited about my wedding—yet there they were making that decision, not for love at the time, but to potentially save their own lives.

I interviewed my parents for this book and asked about their lives and dreams. I am not changing any of their words or correcting their English, except in very minor instances for the sake of clarity on the printed page. The stories they share speak to who my parents are and how strong their resolve must have been. I believe we all wonder what we're made of. What *we* would do when faced with war or famine. Yet, even marrying did not keep them safe. As my mother told me:

> We got married, and then I go to the rice field again, and he stay in the village and grow vegetables until the Vietnamese invaded Cambodia. I didn't know he running away from the soldiers, and he saw me for a little bit, then he go off. I didn't know anything about it. I didn't hear the gunshot in the village because I'm so far out on the farm. And so he go hide in the water where the water lilies [grow]; he hide under those bushes. And stay in the water overnight until the next day because they tried to find him and shoot him.
>
> And so finally, he came back to town. I said, "How come you don't tell me all this stuff?" And I didn't know my brother was out in the stuff too. And we all sleep in a dirt floor. … That's how we got started. And then they all moving us, moving all the family out to a bigger street. They have a street, and we live on just a dirt street on the farm. So they moving to the street, and that's how we are. Just keep going, try to find some place that we are familiar with and start there and pick up some grain of rice on the road and clean up, eat every day, pick up some watergrass, and stuff like that. We can eat on a farm in a rice field, whatever we can find.

The Khmer Rouge was a violent, radical communist movement led by Pol Pot, a man who engineered the genocide of his own people. Some of the first people executed were the educated, the professional and technical classes, and anyone who worked for the former government. Young village people like my parents would most likely be sent to a labor camp, where they would be forced into a form of indentured servitude, working on collective farms without pay, rest, or adequate food. There, most people died, either via execution for not meeting their daily quota on the collective farm or through literal exhaustion, overwork, starvation, or disease.

Consequently, my mother and father married after working in a rice field all day, in the dead of night with a single candle for light. It was not a joyous occasion. In fact, when they got married, my mother slept next to my dad's sister on their wedding night because she didn't even know him.

My parents hadn't been married long when, listening to the radio one afternoon, they heard that the Vietnamese army had invaded Cambodia—more war and trouble. They were between two impossible situations. The Vietnamese would kill them as enemies. And Pol Pot and the regime would kill them through executions and starvation. The situation felt even more urgent. The Khmer Rouge was moving families around, as my mom described. There was less and less food—people were literally looking for dropped grains on the road. My dad and his family knew they were going to try to escape. He told my mother that she could stay with her family if she chose, and he would try to come back and find her one day if he were able. But she elected to go with him—a chance for freedom, a chance for survival, yet into the true unknown with such courage.

My relatives left under the cover of night with the help of a guide. Guerilla soldiers for the Khmer Rouge roamed, and my family needed to stay hidden in the darkness. The jungles of Cambodia are oppressive—thick and claustrophobic. My father, mother, and his immediate family negotiated a minefield. Again, I cannot imagine the heart-pounding terror of crossing such a field in pitch darkness. Against nearly impossible odds, they eventually reached the Thai–Cambodian border.

From there, my family next had to wait some months in a refugee camp to be sponsored. As with most refugee camps, conditions were primitive, and not knowing what would happen next was nerve-racking. Other families had tried to reach Thailand as well—but had been turned away at the border. So even making it that far was a miracle.

My grandfather had heard that the United States was a good place to immigrate to, so he wrote "USA" on a paper with a list of the family members at the camp. However, my grandfather actually drew a line across the paper because there were other family members who wanted to go to Australia, so beneath the line, he listed the family members who wanted to go elsewhere. But my parents' names were listed for the United States. The people running the camp ended up tearing that paper at the line, and the family members who were under the line did not get to leave at that time.

My parents were sponsored by the First Mennonite Church of Berne, Indiana, which I will talk about more in the chapter on faith. Berne is a very small town. When my parents arrived in 1979 at this place they had never seen before (and which was cold!), only about three thousand people lived there—and there are not too many more today. In a mid-Western town dominated by blond people with Swiss heritage, my family were the first Asian refugees to move there. Everything was new and strange—and lonely. In my mother's own words:

> Yes, we had just got married … for a year, yet I came to the United States, left my family and all that. And we [my family] don't see each other until ten years later, and we find each other. It's hard for me to grow up in a new culture. I used to grow up with a family—close-knit too. My mom did not let me go out freely. Here, children go out, and they're by themselves.
>
> So, as my kids grew up more and more, they going to middle school and high school and stuff. It's really, really tough on me

> then because I thought, wow, what happens if my kid do this and do that? I'm always warning them all the time—I'm not supporting you if you do all the bad stuff. So, I keep telling Emily, "You need to just find a good friend. You can find bad friend every corner of the street, everywhere."
>
> I know because I grew up and take care of family and home and all that. So, I don't know. I never have this experience.

My father worked at the local grocery store and also at a factory. My mom worked in a furniture store sewing armrest covers. Because both of my parents were hard workers and quick learners, they were often asked to work extra shifts or stay late. They appreciated their jobs and always took the extra work because they already knew they were saving to buy their first house and their own business.

My paternal grandfather had, before my family's escape, traded across the Thai–Cambodian border, so my dad had an entrepreneurial spirit. My grandfather, early on after they arrived, would ask my father when he was going to start his own business. As a young boy in Cambodia, before the turmoil there, my dad would sell bread that his family had baked before he went to school. Not being shy, he would call out, "Bread! Come buy my bread!" before the sun even rose, and he also made deliveries to regular customers.

My father originally wanted to buy a McDonald's franchise, but he could not obtain a bank loan for that franchise because he could not speak English well. Interestingly, many Cambodian immigrants bought (and still buy) donut shops. (In Southern California, where this tradition began, 80 percent of donut shops are owned by Cambodians.[1]) These small shops have low startup costs, do not require English fluency,

1 Cathy Chaplin, "The Donut Kids Are All Right," *Eater Los Angeles,* June 1, 2022, https://la.eater.com/2022/6/1/23064652/los-angeles-cambodian-doughnut-shops-next-generation.

and are relatively easy for a family or just a couple of people to operate. (As long as you do not mind that seven-days-a-week schedule and hard work—my relatives would definitely not say it is easy. At one point, my parents kept the donut shop open twenty-four hours a day!)

I remember being five or so and riding in the car with my father on the way to the donut shop. As he drove, he told me again, the same lecture, "You should be so grateful you live in the USA."

Like many parents and children on their way to school, we then discussed what I wanted to be when I grew up. I remember telling him that I thought I would be a lawyer because even as a little girl, I argued a lot with my parents. My dad told me there were too many lawyers in the world. He told me I should instead be a doctor—"That way, you will be able to help people."

I still have one of those little construction-paper booklets kids make in school, where there was a line to write what I wanted to be when I grew up, and I wrote in crayon that I want to be a doctor or a lawyer. After that conversation with my father, throughout elementary school, I dropped the lawyer ambition and only wrote that I wanted to be a doctor. I am sure my father, at the time, had no idea what an impact those words would have on me. I thought I wanted to be a pediatrician—I have *always* gravitated toward children and liked to make them smile, able to establish an easy rapport with them.

Later, during my first year at Butler University, I went on a mission trip to Ecuador. I still planned to be a doctor and was premed. On the mission trip, I was there specifically to support the medical team. We set up a type of triage to administer medications to people. However, there was also a dentist on the trip, and I had braces myself at the time. I ended up assisting him with the children, and I loved putting them at ease. I naturally have always loved little kids. The dentist said, "You should really think about going into dentistry instead of medicine."

When I returned to the United States, I gave it some thought. I also shared my experience with my best friend, who was also premed. Then I asked my parents for advice, and my mom said she thought dentistry would be a good choice. The hours would be more stable—a plus if I planned to have a family someday—and I would not have to go to school for quite as long a time as to be a doctor (though it would still take me all of my twenties to achieve my degree and goal). By going into dentistry, I would still be helping people—fulfilling my sense of purpose. And then, over a decade later, there I was taking on huge loans for a practice to run.

But again, I could look to the example of my parents. Coming to the United States and purchasing a business in a year or two was not the only courageous aspect of their journey. In 1979, when my parents arrived, the United States was not kind to Asian refugees. My parents' sponsoring church was amazing—but the country itself had not yet reckoned with the Vietnam War, which had only ended in 1975. The United States had also dropped bombs on Cambodia as well as Laos. Asian immigrants were not welcome.

My mother, ever the person to see a silver lining, says the language barrier helped in that situation because my parents didn't understand what the cruel people who were using slurs or making fun of them were even saying. My mother and father were often made fun of for their eyes or their black hair. (I was the only child with black hair in my school when I was little and occasionally received the same treatment.)

Yet my parents chose never to be bitter and instead chose to be givers, to keep showing up day after day—after day. That's courage. My parents never gave excuses for why they couldn't do things. So making excuses is difficult for me, too, to this day. They've passed that trait on to me as well.

When I was purchasing the practice—essentially signing my life away on those loan papers—I took a deep breath, but I knew, deep down, I could do it. I had seen that entrepreneurial courage in my father—who had seen it, in a different way, but nonetheless that same courage, in his own father. It felt, perhaps, like my whole life was leading to this moment.

And in some ways, it was. My parents would say to me, "You don't want somebody telling you what to do. You don't like it." (Remember, I was the arguer as a child.) "And you wouldn't be good at it." (Also true.) They encouraged me to find a practice that I could buy and thus own my own business. As I wrote earlier, today, most orthodontic graduates do not want the responsibility of owning a business because staff management is the toughest part. You go to school focusing on teeth and braces—only to learn that this is just one aspect of being an orthodontist. In fact, a faculty member during my residency said, "When you get done here, you all think that learning orthodontics is the hard part. But you're going to realize that the orthodontics is the easy part, and it's managing your staff that will challenge you." Thus, not many new graduates are interested in buying practices.

Additionally, similar to most doctors today who are part of massive practices that have holdings all across a state or even the country, there are large groups that are buying up dental practices. In those situations, the doctor essentially turns into the employee of the dental office, which I would absolutely hate. *My parents know me so well.*

So, during my fellowship year, I went and spent time with every single orthodontist in Fort Wayne, Indiana—still in my home state but a bigger city. There were thirteen doctors, and I was trying to figure out if any of them were going to need an associate or if they were approaching retirement or wanted to sell their practice. A couple of doctors wanted an associate doctor. But then I learned that my sister's mother-in-law was working for an orthodontist in Warsaw, Indiana, who was considering retirement.

There were tough back-and-forth negotiations between our lawyers (another skill I did not learn during residency!), to the point that the doctor basically gave me an ultimatum to either buy or not buy the practice, take it or leave it. One week before we signed the papers, I discovered that I was pregnant, but in another bit of courage, I decided to forge ahead with my plan.

I am sure I was every shade of green as I was sick and throwing up at work when pregnant with my daughter, while also trying to learn all the ins and outs of the practice. Not only that, as is sometimes (often) the case, I was dealing with leadership issues right away, as people who had worked for the former orthodontist for years were not quite ready to listen to this young orthodontist fresh out of residency. In fact, I later found out that one of them told the consultant I hired, "She doesn't know what she's doing." (Of course I did.) But I knew I had to show up—and take the leadership reins. I would not be my parents' daughter if I did not!

I was not quite working donut-shop hours—but they weren't too far off. When I was a little girl, I remember sleeping on the sacks of flour in the back office of the donut shop. The orthodontist began his days in the Warsaw office with his first patient at seven in the morning, and conducted his last exam at five in the afternoon. Then there was the satellite office in Plymouth that was about ninety minutes from where I was located in Fort Wayne. (My husband and I were looking for a place more central to both practices.) My husband would get to his office at about a quarter past six in the morning, so I was leaving Fort Wayne at about five each morning—again, pregnant and sick as a dog—to drive to either Warsaw or Plymouth.

When my husband and I did find a house, I would come home at the end of the day and lie on the couch, exhausted to my core and with a trash can next to me in case I got sick. Sometimes, such as when we needed to do the payroll and monthly paperwork, or if the previous orthodontist would want to talk with me a bit more about the practice, wanting to no doubt fill me with all the knowledge of his patients before he retired, I would not get home until eight or even half past eight at night.

There were other things I never considered when I was an orthodontic resident—again, not the clinical aspect, but the "owning a practice" side of things. While pregnant, I would need to show up early to vacuum the carpets or blow leaves off the sidewalk and lawn outside in the fall. I hadn't counted on the mundane parts of being a business owner, yet how many times had I watched my parents wiping down counters and mopping floors? They would also spend the afternoon on Christmas or the day after deep cleaning the donut shop. I would get so frustrated as a child, wondering why they could never take any time off. After becoming a business owner, I understood so much better.

So taking over the practice was not easy. But one thing about watching my parents work seven days a week for decades was that I knew I had to find that inner courage and, honestly, just deal with it. People would not be leaders if they quit when the going got very difficult. My parents had not stopped at a field of buried landmines. I could hardly give up.

The first five *years* of my practice were difficult, awful at times even. Another friend, an orthodontist as well, took me under her wing a bit, and she reassured me that it *is* hard. She shared a conversation she had with herself, the gist of which was that if she continued to be miserable after five years, she was going to sell her practice. This gave me a sense of hope. (I know that sounds a little odd.) The reason it offered hope is that running a practice wasn't what I had envisioned either. So I, too, adopted this line of thinking. Luckily, even though times were tough, each year got better, and so I kept going. Today, I am thrilled with what our practice has achieved.

During hard times, I told myself that it wasn't what I had envisioned, but that was no reason to be discouraged. I am sure that during my parents' first bitterly cold Indiana winter, working in a factory, my father hadn't envisioned his new life looking like that either.

So, I had to find courage even just for the day-to-day things. I am more of an introvert—I don't like being out there in front of people per se—but there's something about being with kids. I love talking to them and making them feel special. I try to make jokes to help them feel comfortable. I absolutely love it, and I seem extroverted when I'm in the office. But when I first came aboard, the retiring doctor was a quieter, more serious orthodontist. The office atmosphere was very focused and professional. There was minimal conversation with patients beyond clinical necessities, mostly just the whirring of equipment. It was certainly quieter than what I had experienced in my residency with my friends, and I found myself being very conscious of how I adapted to this more reserved environment. That was just his style, which was very different from mine. I had grown up seeing my father chat with everyone who came into the donut shop. He was just always outgoing and positive.

When I bought the practice, it still had paper charts—and I charted electronically. The x-rays today are digital—but the previous orthodontist's x-rays were the old film style. In my leadership role, I was trying to figure out what systems to put in place.

The office manager pulled me aside and said, "You can't just come in here and change everything."

I tried to express myself patiently and kindly—while making it clear that we needed to move toward digital and all the advances that were making orthodontics more exciting as a field than ever. My courage as a business owner included doing things my way—not just for the sake of change but for the betterment and modernization of the practice. And it took courage to push against disapproval. I don't thrive on confrontation.

I also took on the renovation of the Plymouth office. To be honest, I tried to not even buy the Plymouth office when I first saw it. It was not in good shape. My father's reaction when he visited once was, "I can't believe people pay you to come see you here."

My mother looked around and said, "It makes me feel itchy in here. You need to find a new place as soon as you can!"

The door that I walked through was so rusted you could see the light through it, and there was a big hole that had developed in the floor where you first walked in. There were traps set to catch critters. Yet that satellite office was my bread and butter for years—it sustained me financially in the beginning, so it was a very good thing I bought it. After a couple of years, I remodeled the Warsaw office. More challenges, more money spent, more stress. Oh, and the blessing of my second pregnancy was during a remodel of my main office.

Eventually, I needed to stop the donut-shop hours. I needed to learn to take vacations and travel. I needed to challenge myself—to not live in a state of constant stress. We'll talk about that journey of mine as we move through the book, but it first began with my parents' courageous journey years ago. I know my own professional journey began with a slightly shaking hand, signing those loan papers. But both then and now, I was filled, thanks to my parents, with an unshakable courage to draw from.

ptember 9, 1980 Vol. 3 No. 19

aing Relatives Arrive

Tears and
fugee famil
eeted by th
out a year a
ny weeks of
ng hope and
The eleven
inesday even
committee m
begger and M
bers Papa a
otions ran h
year-old mo
ir families
people move
e where the
ily were rea
per of heart
iting, crying, and sharing continued
o the early morning hours.
The eleven new Chinese Cambodian
ugees are living in the former Post-
d house, next to the Taing family.
extend them a warm welcome to the
rch and community.

One of the thrilling and ap
features of the Mission Festiv
singing by our Cambodian frien
a fifteen-voice choir they sang
Sheep am I," with feeling and
sh and then in t
closed with the
and learned in
which had bee
eth Huser, who
he Cambodians, se
d Rev. Curt Cla
the piano.

es Bri

BY SHARON LITTLE
and BECKY RICHARDS

Beginning today, the halls and classrooms of Central Catholic High School, closed for school purposes since 1972, will ring again with life — this time with the voices of Indochinese refugees.

Through the efforts of Bishop William McManus, the Diocese of Fort Wayne-South Bend, and Catholic Charities, Vietnamese, Cambodian, Laotian and Hmong refugees will be temporarily housed, dormitory-style, in the now largely unused building at South Clinton and Lewis streets. The Hmong are hill tribesmen in Laos.

Erik Henry, refugee coordinator for Catholic Charities, which began the Indochinese resettlement program four years ago, said eight refugees will be staying at the school beginning tonight and "we are hoping within three weeks to have the total resettlement program (including offices and four staff members) operating out of Central Catholic."

Henry and John Martin, charities director, said in-

creased quotas of the U.S. Immigration and
Service are permitting more of these refug
United States. Henry estimated that 500
will come to this area per month due to the
tas.

Central Catholic will house about 35
time, Henry said. "We are hoping the fami
there for longer than two or three weeks, but
the availability of sponsoring families."

Coming from among
camps awaiting resettlement, they need
training, recreation, space to prepare meals
adjusting to the dramatically different Am
ment.

Martin said the diocese "is not looking
ing into 'Central Catholic hotel,'" but, rathe
city as a logical, convenient site for shelter
while their initial housing and other resettl

Free at last!

Taing relatives begi

CHAPTER 2

Living in Gratitude

At times our own light goes out and is rekindled by a spark from another person. Each of us has cause to think with deep gratitude of those who have lighted the flame within us.

~ ALBERT SCHWEITZER

I think it is remarkable that neither of my parents has a trace of bitterness about what happened to them in Cambodia, despite experiencing the worst of what humans can do to one another during a genocide that lasted for about four years. There is also no bitterness in their hearts over any of the difficulties and trials they experienced in the United States once they arrived. Instead, they walk through the world with gratitude. I appreciate much more now this trait they share, and I try to pass that gratitude on to my daughters. I realize that my girls are growing up with greater privilege than I did, and their experiences are worlds away from my parents', so it is important that they see me model gratitude in all I do.

When my parents came to Indiana, it all felt strange and new to them. They were isolated by not knowing the language and by knowing nothing of the ways of the United States—which to them was just a concept, not "real" until they got here. My father said that he had simply heard in the refugee camp that the United States was the best country! (Something he still believes.) In the States, my family had kind people from the church who drove them to English lessons and helped them navigate this new life, but that new life was still very *hard.* For my mother, she had left her own family, so despite her new marriage to my dad and her friendship with his sister, her experience was even more isolating. Like all refugees, they had deep gratitude for their escape—while at the same time experiencing painful grief and worry over those left behind.

My mom said that during their first winter, they did not even know to wear winter shoes—they had always been barefoot. Though the house where the church put them up had a washer and dryer in the basement, Mom still did the laundry by hand, wringing out clothes the old-fashioned, backbreaking way. It was all she was used to.

Originally, the Mennonite Church that sponsored them put them up in a small house—all of my family together alongside the sponsor family. But by working long hours and multiple jobs, my parents scrimped and saved and paid cash for a trailer of their own to live in, something they could own outright rather than taking on debt by purchasing a house with a mortgage. My father paid cash for his first car, too. Later, when my father bought not only the donut shop but also the building it was in, he paid off the debt he took on from the building owner in just nine years—while still raising a family—by working those long hours and relentlessly paying down that note. He just did not like the feeling of being in financial debt to anyone—not even a bank.

My mother bought all our clothes at the thrift store (where, she brags just a tiny bit, she learned how to shop for good sales), or she made them. I felt guilty for wanting nicer things as a child, wanting to wear what the other kids at school wore—the name brands that were "cool." (My mother recently teased that I still like nice clothes and purses today!) Wearing hand-me-down-type clothing added to my feeling like an outsider. As I said, I was already the only girl with black hair—the only Asian in my school aside from my sister. But now, with the wisdom of an adult, I can also see that my parents sacrificed to make sure my siblings and I had what we needed. I cannot imagine how often they might have gone without to make sure we were cared for.

I understood that I had to work hard in school, and I wanted to make my parents proud of me. But I also had frustrations with how different my life was from my friends' lives. As I mentioned, growing up, my dad worked seven days a week. He would wake up at three or half past three in the morning and go to the donut shop in the dead of night, working until eleven or twelve in the morning. Then, he would come home, eat lunch, take a nap until two or so in the afternoon, and at half past three, leave again until seven, when he came home for dinner. And then he'd sleep a little, then get up again in the middle of the night and do it all over again, seven days a week, 365 days a year.

As I wrote in chapter 1, the donut shop was even open on Christmas Day. My kids are still young enough to believe in Santa and all of the wonders of the season, so we try to keep that magic alive every Christmas. (Maybe because I didn't have Christmases like that, I like the lights and magic and surprises too!) But growing up, I knew my parents bought the presents. I would beg my mother on Christmas morning to let us open the presents early. Every year, the answer was the same—no, you have to wait until your father gets home at noon. Waiting felt excruciating. Meanwhile, my poor father had gotten up at half past three in the cold and dark, just like every other day. (And Christmas Day was the day they deep cleaned the shop, too!)

My parents told me at a very early age that I had to go to school and study hard because they did not want that life for me. My mother would say, "We want you to have a life. We don't want you to have to work this hard seven days a week." Many Cambodian donut shops have gone on to second and even third generations. (In fact, there's been a resurgence through Instagram accounts and the social media savvy of the next generations.) However, my parents did not envision me ever taking over the business. That was not their dream for me.

They had a practicality born of what they had experienced. But, like most kids, I didn't see the whole picture at the time. For me, as I moved into middle and high school, all I knew was that they were very strict—stricter than any other parents I knew. I *was* allowed to do activities such as sports after school, or I could participate in church activities, so I made sure to keep busy so I didn't have to be home or at the donut shop. I played volleyball from middle school through high school year-round, and I know that back then, I resented my father for never making it to a single one of my games because he had to work. Meanwhile, other dads were in the stands cheering us on or even on the sidelines coaching. When I was a teen, I thought it was a choice when my dad was not there—as an adult, I realize it was necessity. It is humbling to think of all of their sacrifices, and today, it fills me with such deep gratitude.

I can count on my hand the number of times that my parents ever went on a true vacation. One time, I asked my father when *our* family would go on a spring break vacation—all my friends took them. Years later, we would travel back to Cambodia as a family, including my daughters, on a true vacation to revisit where our family is from. It was an incredibly special trip that you'll read about later, but back then, when I was young and wanted to fit in with my friends going on spring break, my dad simply responded, "Do you want a house to live in and clothes to wear and food to eat, or do you want to go somewhere for a week?"

Gratitude for Simple Blessings

While I am incredibly grateful for my family and home, for being able to vacation, for owning my practice, for my education and opportunities, I also know from my parents' example that we need to look for blessings and feel gratitude for the little things as much as, if not more than, the big things.

I will talk more about my parents' journey and the church that sponsored them more in the chapter on faith, but in many ways, their story is filled with the "miracles" too many of us discount. Some think of miracles as visions or angels in the sky. In my parents' world, the miracles included escaping with their lives. Some of my family members told stories of stepping on dead bodies as they walked through the fields because they would at least know no land mines were beneath the bodies. Just making it to Thailand was the first miracle.

But the miracles continued when two women clear across the globe saw the plight of refugees and asked their pastor if they could sponsor a family. Strangers far, far away somehow connected with my family and changed their lives—and ultimately my own.

My parents could have chosen to look at their experiences as only loss. They certainly suffered more than their fair share of it. I know people become shriveled and bitter over far, far less. Instead, my parents saw the miracles around them. The blessings and gratitude in things big and small.

For example, my grandfather died of starvation during Pol Pot's reign of terror. This tragedy, of course, impacted my family—even me, who never met him. As I wrote before, we never wasted food in our house, not so much as a grain of rice. It was only right that we should receive the blessings of food with gratitude in our hearts and understand how lucky we were.

With my own daughters, I try to mirror that gratitude. We live in a country of excesses. When I see so much food wasted at restaurants or supermarkets or in people's homes, I am uncomfortable. In our house, if my girls don't finish their supper, sometimes it goes in the fridge to be reheated for when they are ready to eat later. On a level that is appropriate for their age, they understand that part of the family's and our ancestors' story includes starvation and going hungry. It's a personal lesson in our home, but there's a lesson in it for everyone because refugees and their human rights conditions are an ongoing issue all over the world. I know it pains my mother, especially when she sees world crises, knowing that civilians and children are suffering. She and my father find news stories like that so painful. Pictures are beamed onto our newsfeeds and into our living rooms of hungry and injured children, yet the world seemingly has not learned from tragedies and the evils of past wars.

I also know that I watched my parents practice gratitude by giving back to others. Being grateful for what they had meant that they were then willing to share their blessings. My father was—at least according to Mom—too generous an employer at times. He would loan money to seemingly anyone with a sad story. Sometimes, that sad story was true—sometimes, I was not so sure. But, regardless, my father is a man with a good heart. My mother got involved in our church, and she, too, was and is a generous person. Whether it was donating food (she likes to introduce people to Chinese cuisine—and she is an amazing cook) or donuts or giving of her time, my mother is so grateful for the blessings in her life that she projects that outward.

In my own life, I think that gratitude comes out particularly in my connection with children in my practice. I want them to feel special, to know that they are safe and that I'm going to ensure they have a beautiful smile—and have a *positive* experience at the orthodontist. I am grateful for my connection with them, grateful for the way I was raised, and I am grateful that deep down, I know who I am because of my parents.

As a leader at work, I know that expressing gratitude and focusing on the positive means a healthier culture. I like to think that our practice is a happy place to work, where people are appreciated for the unique gifts they bring to us each day—their strengths.

American Dream

I know my parents are grateful for their children and grandchildren. They beam when they talk about them. They are grateful for their faith. But the other thing I believe they deeply treasure is the American Dream. Our family is the living embodiment of that.

Again, as an impatient (and maybe just a touch impertinent) child, I thought my father was a bit of a broken record—*how lucky we are, how lucky we are to live in this great country.* My guess is I may have rolled my eyes a few times. If you are the only kid who is never allowed to go to a sleepover, you don't necessarily feel lucky. You don't always feel lucky sleeping on a flour sack in the back of a donut shop, wanting to be home in your own bed.

However, my father just humbly persevered—and feels grateful despite the hardships. When I asked him about the American Dream, he said:

> Well, I always say you come to the United States, the opportunity [is there] for you. The opportunity [is there] for you, but you have to fight for it! Nobody give it to you. You have to work hard for it. If you think about when we live in Cambodia, I go to work every morning, every day for my dad. So, if you train yourself, work hard, you always [have] success.
>
> But [if] you don't want to work ... you just lay on the couch, wait, wait for the food to fly in. It not going to happen. And I work 365 days a year. Maybe Thanksgiving, I closed, but I still go clean the donut shop. I make sure the place clean. Working. My dad always say, working is not going to kill you. You don't have food. You don't eat. That kill you. ... And I make sure they [my children] all go to school. I keep telling them, make sure you go to school, because you want to become somebody. You have to straight out yourself. Don't go do drugs; don't go and smoke. Don't go drink. But they listen, though. They listen.

I did listen!

I knew my education was part of that American Dream. I needed to have gratitude for that as well. One time in elementary school, I got a lone B+. My dad had questions about that—why the B+? I therefore knew I would *not* be bringing home anything other than A's ever again.

Another time, I did not do very well on a test I took for social studies. When it was time for the next social studies test, I remember so vividly sitting down in the living room and just reading and reading and reading the same chapter over and over and over again until I had practically memorized it word for word. And then, I went to take the next test, and it was so easy for me. I got the A+. That was about the third grade—and it made a big impact on me. As my father said, *you* can make yourself successful with hard work. I saw firsthand that, with the American Dream, anything was possible. With my own daughters, I want them to try their best, and if they get a grade less than what they are capable of, I encourage them to do as I did and study until it's easy. I made very good grades all through high school, college, and beyond, but I would never want to give the impression that it did not take a lot of effort. Hard work is OK.

My mom did not get to finish school. In fact, neither of my parents were able to complete their education. My mom struggled with numbers when they first started their business—she had not had the opportunity for a formal education, and math was difficult for her. Like many immigrant families, I think there is also a certain competition, if you will, for the first-generation kids to do their very best. I knew at a very young age that B's (or, heaven forbid, worse!) were shameful in our family. My mom taught me to focus on working hard and not to worry if other kids occasionally made fun of me for being a top student. She remembered, recently, some advice she once gave me: "I said when you go to school, and I think that's why you always get straight A. … I said, you think about people making fun of you; you think about it. Is that person smarter than you?" In other words, we all know that sometimes the smart kids—whether a generation calls them nerds or geeks or brainiacs—are made fun of. But she was reminding me that the smart people would be fine and to ignore anyone who would tease me.

My parents would remind my sister and me that we live in a country where you get to go to school for free. I understood that I could not let that go to waste or care what anyone else thought of us. My mom and dad would tell me to attend school until I couldn't go to school anymore—to get the highest degree possible I could and then do something to help people. They instilled in me that I should not take these opportunities for granted and should be grateful for them. These principles are ingrained within me—in my practice, we even have a book club because we should never stop learning. My dad always said he could not understand people who are born in the United States and yet don't realize or appreciate the many opportunities they have.

I asked my mother about how she felt when I went off to college (really, my first taste of freedom after growing up in a strict immigrant family). She said, "I told you the same thing. I keep telling you again. I said, 'I cannot see you, but God can see you. Whatever you do, remember, don't just tell me what I want to hear. You go to Boston … you spend a lot of money. You borrow money to go to school and college, too, and … if you want to go party and drinking and throw yourself away, then forget it. Just stay home.'"

I did set off for the big, wide world outside Berne, Indiana. But the amazing thing about the gratitude I felt deep down inside, and my understanding of my parents' sacrifices, was that I ultimately wanted to return to them and that I learned to lean on them, to see their wisdom and how it applied to life. So when it was time to buy my practice, Indiana was home.

Gratitude Today

The beginning of my career was so difficult that I often say there could be no way that I could have a workday now that could *possibly* be as bad as it was then (not that I want to tempt fate!). A satellite office in disarray and disrepair (I shudder at the critter traps), not all employees welcoming me as a new doctor (let alone a new doctor who wanted to modernize and change things and create new systems and efficiencies), feeling sick every day from my pregnancy, overwhelmed not just by the immense debt and challenges I'd taken on, on top of everything else I had to learn as I acquired the practice—oh, *and* all while not having a house convenient to the offices and working donut-shop hours. If I could have, before all of this, made a list of ten incredibly stressful things that could go wrong when buying a medical practice—while pregnant—I am pretty sure I could have checked off all ten by the time all was said and done.

Anytime little or big difficulties happen in life, whenever I am facing something tough, I lean into my faith and gratitude and the lessons I learned from my parents. My mom instilled in us the idea that God saved my parents from the war for a reason. Consequently, I have strong faith that whatever happens, happens for a reason. Therefore, I try to maintain my sense of gratitude.

I also, in a practical sense, ask myself in any negative situation, "Is there something that I can change?" If I can, then I do so. And if I can't, I let it go. That helps me shed many unnecessary stresses. There is enough to worry about in the things we can control—so I leave the things I can't control up to God.

There is an ever-present aspect of mental health to consider when owning your own business. It can be so all-consuming—as I am sure any entrepreneur reading this knows. I saw it with my own parents. Whatever situations I have going on in my practice, I stop and consider how I can make them better. Whatever the drama (and there will always be drama in any place of employment), whether it is people leaving or scheduling issues, I want to know how I am going to make it easier for the team. I lean toward "What are we going to do?" versus panic. Instead of dwelling on something that happened that was out of my control, I ask myself, "What is something actionable I can do that will impact the situation?"

I have learned to respond, not react.

Here, again, I am grateful for the lessons others have taught me. My husband is a firefighter/paramedic, and I see how stressful his job is in comparison to my own. At least I know in my case that nobody's life is on the line. I always tell my staff, even though something might seem like a big deal, nobody's dying. I try to help them see any setback or office crisis in a different light. Sometimes, we need perspective. I need only look to my parents anytime I need a reminder of all I should be grateful for—and all I should not worry about.

We can take the view that even the difficult days are part of life, and we can be grateful for the lessons we learn in trying times. Even during the hard times, we need to look for the gifts. Sometimes, it's important to stop and see the things we take for granted—such as food on the table or our education and all that we learned that cannot be taken away from us.

Gratitude is important because it allows us to shift our focus from what we lack to what we have. I have seen people I know become broken by bitterness; I've seen it lead to addictions to gambling, drugs, or alcohol. I try to keep my sense of wonder about me, that appreciation my dad tried to drill into me: *How lucky we are. How lucky we are.*

I know that when I practice gratitude, I am able to respond and not react. I don't have to lose my personal sense of serenity that I can draw from like a well, from both faith and gratitude. That is a gift in a world filled with people who will lose their serenity over losing a parking spot or waiting ten minutes for a table at a restaurant.

Later in the book, I will talk more about *StrengthsFinder 2.0*—but one of my strengths is Harmony. I don't think you can have harmony without gratitude. I saw firsthand that grateful people, such as my parents, are better able to handle adversity because they focus on the positive aspects of their lives. Letting go of negativity, cultivating gratitude, knowing who I am at my core, leading with empathy—these all work together to create the kind of practice, life, and family I want to have.

ptember 9, 1980 Vol. 3 No. 19
aing Relatives Arrive
Free at last!
Taing relatives begi

CHAPTER 3

The Value of Hard Work and Tenacity

Always bear in mind that your own resolution to succeed is more important than any other.

~ ABRAHAM LINCOLN

My parents' first home—one that they owned free and clear—was that trailer I talked about in chapter 2 that they paid $2,000 cash for. It may have been drafty in the winters and not fancy, but I am prouder of them for buying that trailer than if we had lived in a castle. I often sit back and think about what they have achieved in their lifetimes.

In *one* generation—their own—they escaped war and starvation to come to a new country that previously hadn't even been a concept to them. While some people accepted them, my parents also encountered racism and cruelty. They went on to buy that humble—but entirely their own—trailer with cash, became small business owners (and, in turn, bought the building the donut shop was in), and became part of the fabric of the town to which they were brought, while not knowing a soul.

As a first-generation American, I was able to go to college and then continue on to dental school, which finally culminated in me pursuing one of the most competitive specialties of my field—orthodontics. Rather than work for someone else, I took on my own business. Though, admittedly, donuts and braces are pretty different!

Growing up, my father would always talk about us kids to his customers at the donut shop. My dad's English may not be perfect, but he is the consummate salesman—not in a smarmy way, but in the sense that he's a genial person who will chat with anyone or lend a helping hand to anyone. He is authentic; his smile is genuine. So, behind the counter at the donut shop, he would brag about us to whomever would listen. He was just so proud that we got to go to school and that we did well in school and went on to college and so on. I try to imagine my father at the age I was then; our experiences and worlds could not have been more different.

Today, if I go into the donut shop, sometimes, a customer will stop me in the doorway or at the counter and say, "Oh, are you one of Ty's daughters?" Or they'll say, "You must be the doctor." And then they will sweetly repeat some story or another that my father told them. I am always touched to know he is proud of me.

Understanding Hard Work Now

Growing up, I think I resented the donut shop (even though I did love donuts). In some ways, it took my parents from me. It was hard as a child not to see the shop as the most important thing to my parents.

Something that's really interesting to me is that, as a child, and still to this day, my parents and I do not say "I love you" to each other, and they do not hug me. That was difficult for me when I was young. Obviously, from the people around us to people on television shows I watched, other families didn't look like mine—or act like mine. I really did feel, at times, that my parents did not love me.

If we were fighting about something (and again, I was Ms. Argumentative), I would sometimes say, "You don't even love me!" (I think every kid has said this in some fashion.)

Their answer was often, "Of course, we love you. Look at all these things that we do for you."

I believe, like many immigrants who must come to the States and claw out a life from scratch, from nothing, that driven nature to work—and the fact that the work available to immigrants is often low-paying and difficult—is sometimes difficult for their children to understand. The parents see the sacrifice and multiple jobs or long hours as providing and showing love. The kids may not see it that way—they just know Mom and Dad are always working. They aren't in the stands at the game. They expect their children to pitch in around the house or in the business. And, as each generation becomes more blended into the culture, relationships change.

I am sure that the fact that my parents were torn away from their lives and country meant that they were not allowed to fully express that love. They showed their love by working hard to provide. *That* was the tangible sign of their love, the proof. Over time, I came to understand this, and I have profound gratitude for their sacrifices.

As such, it is so gratifying and beautiful for me to see my parents with my own kids now. I watch them give my children hugs all the time and tell them that they love them. I feel honored and blessed to witness this experience. I treasure watching them together. At last,

I get to see my parents relax a little and spoil their little princesses. (My mom, for instance, will cook them any Chinese dish they want.)

It's funny to see how different we really are, generation from generation, when I watch my parents with my girls. One time, when one of my little ones was in kindergarten, there was the typical end-of-year excitement when those little angels are hopped up on cupcakes and classroom excitement. One of my daughters was just a bit too rambunctious—and so she ended up in the principal's office twice in one week.

When I got home at the end of the workday, my parents were there babysitting (it truly does take a village for working parents—more on this later!), and I took my daughter into her room to discuss her behavior.

I sat her on her bed, and she told me what happened. Very solemnly, doing my best stern-mom face, I informed her that, one summer, my parents (she calls my mother Ama and my father Kong) did not let me do a single thing. "All summer, the only thing I could do was sit on Ama and Kong's bed and watch TV. That was it. No outside time. Nothing," I said. "And if I get one more bad report about you from school, I'm going to make your summer just like that. Is that what you want?"

My daughter looked pretty shocked. We ended things with a hug, but not before we had a whole conversation about expectations and how she had to behave in school.

My parents heard all of it through my daughter's cracked bedroom door, and when I emerged, my father said to me, "It's OK, Emily. She's all right."

My mom pulled me aside to offer this advice: "Don't be too hard on her. You want to be firm, but not too firm. You have to be understanding. You have to be right in the middle."

All I could think was, *Who are you people?!*

I can remember my parents very specifically telling me not to embarrass myself or the family. I was told I could not get in *any* trouble at school. I could not do this and could not do that. When I was a teenager, the expectation was that I would never date.

I believe I am now a bridge between my parents' lessons and the lessons I want to pass along to my girls in my own way. For example, I do make my daughter work to memorize or read over and over to get her spelling words correct. I tell her the story of that social studies test. I also tell her that, though I went to dental school, it was not as if it came easily to me. I try to show her that the hard work pays off with a good grade.

But I don't think my kids resent my orthodontic practice like I sometimes resented the donut shop. I try to be there for their important school things, to take them to church—and we get to open Christmas presents before noon. My practice is also filled with kids and is a happy place to be. In fact, one of my girls says she wants to be an orthodontist and work with me "so we can go out for lunch together." Little does she know how hard the work can be—but also how rewarding.

As a leader, I try to be an empathetic boss—my employees are mostly women, and many are moms. We all want to be at school events; we all face having kids sent home from school with the sniffles. However, I think my biggest lesson was learning to be empathetic with myself. I still have to work on that sometimes. The "hard-work gene" is pretty strong in me. And when I first started my practice, there were some grueling years. But I increasingly see—with my village to help me—the importance of ensuring I schedule time off or plan fun events. When I take care of myself, I'm a better leader to everyone else.

The Immigrant Work Ethic

As a first-generation American with a front-row seat to the challenges that come with maintaining a work–life balance—as well as the power that a relentless work ethic brings with it—being the daughter of immigrants has informed so much of my life.

I said this earlier, but for my parents, their work ethic was born out of necessity first and ambition second. They needed to be able to support themselves in their new country, so they started with factory work—where it wasn't necessary to be fluent in English to work with the machines—and took extra shifts whenever they could. Anything to work more and save more.

Lin-Manuel Miranda even wrote the song "Immigrants (We Get the Job Done)" in tribute to that work ethic and to the people who came to these shores and took on the hard jobs, because those were the jobs that would hire them.

But maybe necessity and ambition are like the chicken and the egg riddle. You've heard about how my father sold bread as a boy, waking in the middle of the night to earn extra money by selling fresh bread loaves his family had baked before heading off to school. And about how his father did some import–export trading across the border with Thailand.

My father was not going to remain in a factory forever—it wasn't what he was destined for—so he worked even harder to get the money to purchase a business without an education and without speaking the language, but with an unshakable work ethic and a faith in God and the American Dream. He was fortunate that the stranger he married—my mother—is also an incredibly hard worker with a will of steel.

But there's a twist. (Isn't there always?) Difficulty returned. Why? Because my father could not get a loan because his English was not strong enough. However, let's be frank. At that time in America, no bank was going to loan money to an Asian immigrant. Thankfully, again, our church came to the rescue, and one of the men from the congregation—the husband of one of the women who had first wanted to sponsor a refugee family—helped him secure a loan.

My family's story is an echo of many. America has been a place of immigrants and a refuge for the war-ravaged. It has a complicated past, but for my family, it has offered us both safety and success.

For most immigrants, their experience is often one of sacrifice, resilience, and tireless effort to create a better life for themselves and their hopes for future generations. The inherent challenges faced by immigrants push them to work harder than many others, not only to survive, but to thrive—just like my parents.

Tenacity and Resilience

I do not know what makes one person crumble in a time of crisis and another rise. I suppose most leaders and leadership books try to dissect that. I just know that when times are difficult, I have a steel backbone. And that backbone probably came from my mother and father.

The resilience of immigrants inspires me. Immigrants remind us all that success is not handed to us but is earned through hard work, sacrifice, and determination.

For example, one of the greatest challenges immigrants face is overcoming language barriers. The church that sponsored our family drove them to and from English lessons that were about forty-five minutes away. Most English as a second language (ESL) classes for new immigrants and refugees are like "survival English." They teach students the very basics to navigate life in their new country—key words and phrases to use at the bank and the grocery store, how to count money, how to fill out a job application, and some basic phrases. Over time, the classes begin to focus on the nuances of the English language.

My parents' English is still a little broken, though no one would have any difficulty understanding them. But when they first arrived, nothing was familiar, and it took tenacity and grit to learn English. But language is *everything* when you are an immigrant.

From the grocery store to driving (remember, this was before GPS—they had to read the road signs!) to operating an oven to understanding how a paycheck works and how to deposit it, there was nothing familiar—not even the landscape or the weather—about Berne, Indiana. Plus, there was no existing community of Cambodian immigrants to help ease the way.

Despite how difficult it was, they committed themselves to learning the language of their host country as quickly as possible. This willingness to learn and adapt is another hallmark of my parents' resilience and tenacity. Part of the reason my dad would talk to anyone and everyone at the donut shop was so he could practice his English skills. And now, he views strangers as just friends he hasn't met yet.

Even when my parents bought the shop, there were complications beyond the language and the finances. As my dad tells the story of the process of purchasing the shop from the seller:

> He told me he must sell this donut shop here because "My wife moved to Texas. If I don't sell the shop, she going to divorce me." I said, "Well, I buy it from you, but I don't have no experience for the donut shop, and could you help me, train me?" He said, "Yeah, I train you for six weeks." I said, "Well, six weeks. I don't think I have enough time, but it's OK. I take six weeks, but you make sure you train me." Then, he train me for one week. He left me. He left me to [go to] Texas.

One week—after my father had just spent all he had to buy the place. But tenacity is something that both my parents have. Dad told my mom:

> "Well, now we have to do it because nobody help." Nobody know [though] that I have my brother that can help me. So we worked five hours each person; my wife worked five hours. "Oh my gosh. Can we keep the business going?" And my sponsor from Mennonite Church, they see, they say, "You have to do it." He say, "You need some help?" I said, "No, I got somebody help me. We got the baker ..." He said, "It's OK, we can do it." And then we work [to] bake the donut, and ... the business good, make good money.

I still am not sure how they pulled it off!

But when it comes to tenacity and resilience, I think the story that comes to mind for me is when my parents located my grandmother (my mother's mother)—years after the war had ended. First, what were the chances she was alive—and then, how would they find her?

My parents sold that first donut shop in their quest to find my grandmother. A friend of my father's had been interested in buying the shop. My father and mother were anxious to try to track down missing family members, and so my father negotiated a selling price that doubled their money and covered what they still owed. This way, they could use some of the profits to go to Thailand to see if they could locate my maternal grandmother.

In my mind, still, when I hear my parents tell the story, it seems like a needle-in-a-haystack situation. My mother had heard rumors that her mom had made her way to Thailand. It was the logical choice for anyone wanting to escape Cambodia. The truth of it was far more complicated.

There was no internet back then to spread the word and ask for help looking for loved ones people had become separated from. My parents had copies made of a photo of themselves, taken before they left Thailand, with their names and contact information and the names of the family members they were trying to find. People were making money from helping to reunite family members—almost like a bounty.

In Thailand, my parents began by searching the refugee camps. Though the wars were largely over, there were still thousands and thousands of refugees and displaced people from various wars in Asia. They were hoping to make their way to the United States or another host country.

By this time, there were fewer camps in Thailand—one "in town," as my mother puts it, and then two farther away. She and my father searched all three, showing their picture around, telling people the names of their missing family members, and asking if any of them had been seen, but to no avail.

But again, my parents are clever, resilient, and tenacious. They heard of someone who was smuggling small items—nothing too big to call attention—from Thailand *back into* Cambodia to help the people there. My parents gave this person their picture and the name of my grandmother to ask around in Cambodia and try to locate her.

One year later, after my parents returned to the States, someone called and said he believed that he had found my grandmother and that she had returned to her home village. From that point on, my parents focused their efforts on trying to get word to her—to let her know that they were searching for her and that they were safe in the United States. Alas, in the process, my mother was informed that her eldest brother had died—he had been murdered for his bike.

My parents urged my maternal grandmother to arrange to get to a refugee camp in Thailand—which turned out to be her second time going to a camp. In fact, my mom learned later on that while she and my dad were at the refugee camp in 1979 before coming to the States, my grandmother had also tried to make it to the border via a van, but it had been stopped by Vietnamese soldiers. The refugees had been released into the jungle and shot at, escaping with their lives but not their freedom. It must have been terrifying, but my grandmother was determined to try to get the family to the border again.

After my parents had located her and urged her to again make the journey to a refugee camp, one of my uncles said he did not want to take the risk of being killed in the jungle to come to the United States. My grandmother still wasn't deterred and decided to go with one of my aunts and another uncle. My mom said that soldiers were being paid a thousand dollars per person to shepherd people through the jungle. A group of three soldiers guided my grandmother and relatives to Thailand, and my parents paid the guides once they reached the border. One of the soldiers stepped on a land mine and bled out and died. Mom said my grandmother was deeply saddened by this because she knew that this was someone else's son who had died. War is indiscriminate. The rest of the group buried him and eventually made it to the border.

By this time, it was 1989, and my parents were able to sponsor my grandmother to come join us in the United States. My dad returned to Thailand to confirm our family members were at the camp and to pay the people who had gotten them to the camp. When I asked my dad what his reaction had been to seeing my grandmother, aunt, and uncle, he broke down in tears. At one point in the conversation, my dad said, "It's a miracle we're here, Emily."

But there is yet another miraculous twist.

Pastor Claussen of their Mennonite Church had a son, Eldon, who had just finished his nursing degree and was preparing to be a missionary. My paternal grandmother told David Chiu—another missionary, based in Goshen, Indiana, who spoke Cantonese and who would translate sermons for my family on Sundays—that she, too, was looking for her mother (my great-grandmother) and sisters, which David then translated to Eldon.

When Eldon went to Cambodia on his mission, he, like my parents, took a photo with my grandmother's name and family information. Eldon found my great-grandmother and great aunts in a refugee camp, and they were sponsored to come to the United States as well.

I kept saying, how did he know where they were? How did he find them specifically? A needle in the haystack or the grace of God.

It is an extraordinary story of tenacity and sheer will. My family never gave up despite unfathomable odds.

Resilience and Tenacity Today

I might joke and say that tenacity was being in a long-distance relationship with my husband—including after we were married—for *years.* Or that tenacity was marrying him despite both my parents' objections. (They wanted me to wait until after I finished my orthodontic residency—but they adore him today.)

But for me, I think I demonstrate tenacity most in my leadership. It is different for women—especially if you look youthful. People, as I found out when I bought the practice, do not necessarily afford you respect when you are a younger leader—they almost expect you to mess up, to fail.

But then I think of that donut shop owner leaving my father after only a week of training—and my family's sponsor saying that my parents *had* to make the donut shop work. By that point, my parents were deeply invested. Failure was never an option. Nor has it been for me.

The lessons I learned about hard work, tenacity, and resilience from my parents and my family's experiences are something I apply every day in my life now. I want to explore some of the top qualities that my family have passed on to me, including adaptability, optimism, problem-solving, and the ability to learn from setbacks and value hard work.

Adaptability

Resilient people are flexible in their thinking and approach. They are open to change and can adjust their strategies when things don't go as planned. I am not sure many things went as planned for my parents. But they persevered. As I wrote earlier, I never expected to be leaf-blowing the outside of the building I bought—but we grab that leaf blower and adapt! Every person holding this book will, at some point in their career, have to adapt to change.

Adaptability has been a constant companion throughout my life, a necessary skill honed by the unique circumstances of my upbringing and career. My parents' journey from war-torn Cambodia to the United States instilled in me a deep understanding of the need to adjust, to pivot, and to embrace change, even when it's uncomfortable.

My parents exemplify adaptability. They left their homeland, learned a new language, embraced a different culture, and worked tirelessly to build a new life for our family. They didn't complain, even when faced with difficulties, which taught me to show up every single day.

This never-give-up attitude, deeply rooted in their faith and gratitude, became a core value that shaped my own approach to life.

Their story taught me that adaptability isn't just about surviving; it's about thriving. It's about recognizing opportunities, even in the face of adversity, and having the courage to pursue them. My father, despite not speaking the language of his new country or having an MBA, possessed an innate gift for connecting with people, which enabled him to be successful in business.

My career as an orthodontist has also demanded a high degree of adaptability. I had to adapt to new technologies, changing patient needs, and the challenges of running a business. When I bought my practice, I didn't even know how to use the equipment in the office (because, frankly, it was outdated, and we needed new technology!). Not to mention the fact that I was pregnant at the time and quickly had to adapt to the responsibilities of being a business owner while managing the physical challenges of pregnancy.

Optimism

Resilient individuals maintain a positive outlook, even when facing significant challenges, even when the going gets tough. I can think of nothing more horrifying than my parents' experiences and those of other displaced people because of the brutality of war. Resilient people believe in their ability to overcome obstacles and that things will eventually improve.

Now, I will be honest—my parents were worriers during my childhood and adolescence (and still are today). Can you blame them? Their very government murdered over a million of its citizens. The United States was filled with opportunity—but also hardships. And, because my parents wanted nothing but the best for me, they were worriers about the temptations of American life—like I said, they were strict! But they have always had a faith that imbues them with optimism. They always tell me, "Don't worry, Emily; it will all work out." And I have learned that optimism and gratitude help me be a resilient leader in the face of tough days.

Problem-Solving

Rather than becoming overwhelmed by adversity, resilient and tenacious people actively seek solutions. They take steps to address problems, break them down into manageable parts, and work toward resolution. I saw my parents try all sorts of things (such as buying a second shop, staying open 24/7 for a time, and so on) to keep their business running well and making money to support us all. One reason I hired a consultant for my practice was to be certain I was attacking the problems of running a thriving business with the best leadership tools I could have in my toolbox.

Problem-solving has become an essential skill in both my personal and professional lives. Whether it's navigating the challenges of running an orthodontic practice, balancing work and family, or simply dealing with everyday issues, I've learned that a proactive and thoughtful approach can make all the difference.

Growing up, I watched my parents overcome incredible obstacles. These lessons instilled in me a deep belief that problems are not insurmountable and that there is always something I can do to make a situation better. My parents' faith also gave them strength to persevere through the trials in their life.

As a business owner, I'm constantly striving to make the best use of my time. That means creating systems that streamline processes and improve efficiency while delegating tasks that others can handle and focusing on activities that only I can do.

Learning from Setbacks

The best leaders learn from setbacks and don't allow setbacks to deter them. I think of my father and the refusal of banks to loan him money on his own—yet he just doubled down on his efforts and, with the help of a congregant from his church, was able to pursue his dream. I have had setbacks in my practice as well—including my practice manager leaving (which, in the end, was a good thing because I could hire a manager who shared my vision for my practice). But the practicality and tenacious spirit of my parents help me. I do not have time for self-pity—instead, I roll up my sleeves, learn from setbacks, and come out the other side stronger and wiser.

Setbacks are an inevitable part of life, both personally and professionally. Whether it's a challenge in my orthodontic practice, a family issue, or something completely unexpected, I've learned that the key to moving forward is how you respond. Drawing on my experiences and the values instilled in me by my parents, I've developed a framework for recovering from setbacks that emphasizes faith, gratitude, resilience, and a proactive approach.

Faith is my mom always telling me that things will work out. Gratitude reminds me to look at a setback through the lens of remembering all of the incredible gifts I have, from food and a roof over my head to personal safety and living in a place where I can send my children to school—and, the fact that they can experience a joyful childhood, unlike the horrors my family faced in Cambodia.

I also believe in taking a proactive approach to problem-solving. I always ask myself, "Is there something that I can change about this situation?" If the answer is yes, I take action. If the answer is no, I try to accept the things I cannot control and focus on what I can control—and learn from all of it.

By embracing these principles, I've been able to navigate challenges and emerge stronger. I believe that setbacks are not roadblocks but rather stepping stones on the path to success. They provide opportunities to learn, grow, and develop the resilience and tenacity needed to achieve your goals.

The Value of Hard Work

As I wrote earlier in this book, hard work is often not glamorous. But I saw firsthand that the value of hard work extends beyond just the tangible outcomes it produces. Hard work fosters resilience, discipline, and self-reliance. It shapes character.

For me, my parents' example shaped who I am as a leader, as a doctor, as a mother, and as a wife. Again, I like to think of myself as a generational bridge. I am grateful to not live in the fear my parents did and that I can now adjust their lessons of hard work to apply them to my own world—and the world of my girls and the next generation to come.

Hard work is more than just putting in hours; it's a foundational principle that has shaped my life and career. A strong work ethic continues to drive me today, one of discipline and recognizing the importance of showing up every day. Even when my father was sick, he would only sleep for a couple of hours and then go back to work. This commitment wasn't about being a workaholic; it was about honoring his responsibilities and providing for his family.

I have always defaulted to that ethic of my dad showing up every single day, and I'm committed to instilling these values in my own children. (And they love their grandparents so much, so it's extra special!) But the tenacity and resilience I learned from my parents are only part of what sustained them through their darkest days. Their unwavering faith provided another source of strength that would prove essential in their journey—and eventually in mine.

cember 9, 1980 Vol. 3 No. 19

ing Relatives Arrive

ears and smiles min
gee families and "g
ted by the Taing fa
t a year ago. The
weeks of waiting,
hope and disappoin
he eleven persons w
esday evening at the
ommittee members Wa
gren and Maggie Lied
ers Paul and Mama Ta
ions ran high as Mam
ear-old mother and
n families. Returni
people found they we
where the remainder
ly were ready with a
er of hearty Chinese
ting, crying, and sha
the early morning ho
e eleven new Chinese
gees are living in th
house, next to the T
xtend them a warm wel
h and community.

One of the thrilling and spec
features of the Mission Festival
singing by our Cambodian friends
a fifteen-voice choir they sang
Sheep am I," with feeling and en
English and then in the
They closed with the do
Chinese and learned in s
gee camp which had been t
Mary Beth Huser, who ha
with the Cambodians, serv
ber, and Rev. Curt Claass
ted at the piano.

gees Brin

Free at last!

Taing relatives begin

CHAPTER 4

The Power of Faith

There were many dark moments when my faith in humanity was sorely tested, but I would not and could not give myself up to despair. That way lays defeat and death.

~ NELSON MANDELA

My own story will forever be inextricably linked to my parents' and extended family's desperate escape from Cambodia and their subsequent courageous journey to the United States. As their daughter, their example guides me. Woven into their story of survival, resilience, and eventual success as small business owners is a profound thread of faith. For my parents, after they came to the United States, faith was not merely a religious affiliation but a source of strength, a beacon of hope, and an unwavering compass guiding them through the trials of being immigrants in a strange new world.

Their experiences, deeply rooted in the horrors of the Khmer Rouge regime and the uncertainty of refugee life, forged in them a unique perspective on faith that profoundly shaped my upbringing and worldview. I saw my father's example of Christian generosity and care for others as well as his gratitude for our lives, even the difficult parts. I saw my mother's example of her reliance on faith and her natural kindness. The church I grew up in—and which embraced my family—became a place where they could express their gratitude, find solace, and cultivate hope, making it a pivotal part of our family life.

The church became a haven for my family, helping us navigate the complexities of American life, find work, and build new relationships. It was the church that rescued my parents and extended family from the refugee camp and brought them to the United States, undoubtedly shaping their perspective on faith. This transition was more than a shift in religious affiliation and adopting Christianity; it was a deepening of their personal relationship with God and reliance on faith in times of trouble.

Looking back, the church showed us what loving the stranger really means.

I am also able to see that my parents gave me such a wonderful example of how a person of faith should behave. My parents are givers. Throughout my life, I have seen them help others in need. If employees or relatives wanted to borrow money from my dad, he never hesitated (to the point that my mom and I both think some of them took advantage of his giving nature). My mother gives through volunteering—and the food she cooks. In so many cultures, food is a sign of love and nurturing. My own daughters have their Cambodian favorites (they love spring rolls), and as a nurturing grandmother, my mother will always prepare them.

The lessons I learned at our first church continue to shape my faith journey today. At my current church, I've found a community that shares the same calling to care for others, particularly those most vulnerable. I'm especially drawn to helping women and vulnerable children in crisis situations. They don't get to choose the circumstances they are in. They are simply forced to do whatever they can to survive. Their stories echo the experiences of my parents and all of the choices they did not get to make, the circumstances that forced them to make impossible choices and undertake a perilous escape. When I work with these vulnerable populations today, I'm honoring my family's history and expressing my profound gratitude to those church members who, decades ago, extended their hands to welcome strangers from across the world. Those strangers' selfless generosity changed not only my parents' lives but mine as well, creating a legacy of compassion that continues to guide me.

As I was writing this book, I realized that my story cannot be separated from theirs, for the threads of their resilience, determination, and faith are tightly woven into the fabric of my identity. Their escape from a brutal regime, their survival against unimaginable odds, and their eventual success as small business owners form the bedrock of my understanding of perseverance and faith.

My Mother's Faith amid the Khmer Rouge's Reign of Terror

My mother's faith story is both harrowing and inspiring, as it emerged from the depths of one of the darkest chapters in modern history. During the Khmer Rouge regime, our family was torn apart and subjected to forced labor, starvation, and the constant fear of death. My mother endured immense suffering: separation from her parents, grueling working conditions, and illness—including malaria. She had no reason to believe she could survive such an ordeal, yet in her despair, she turned to prayer. With no prior knowledge of Christianity or its teachings, she prayed with a plea from her soul. Here are her own words:

> My mom sent me to the jungle here to cut up some grass to build a roof. And I was out on the field, and I don't know my way around sometime. I kind of felt lost, and later on, when it's hard, you work so hard, you don't have enough to eat. And I thought in my mind, I thought I'm going to die. I don't think I'm going to make it just so weak. … And so I do pray and said in Cambodia's Buddha and I do pray a lot, and I said, if there's a God somewhere, deliver me out from here. That could be my God. So, this is so hard because people sick and die. And I came to the camp; we do read a book about … I don't [know] the book about talking about the straight way and the crooked way.
>
> I don't remember what the book was called, but in Cambodia, I just read it because I was in a camp, and they talk about the straight way. It take longer to go somewhere that you want to be, in heaven or something; this man here and tell his son or children that don't go this way—just take time and go to the straight way. Don't go crooked way. You go in the ditch and all that fall off the road. And then, I don't know what happened when I came to United States; I saw the big church. I thought that's a king palace.

At the time, my mother's family practiced Buddhism, and she had no concept of the Christian God. Yet, in that pivotal moment, she felt a profound sense of divine intervention—a glimmer of hope that carried her through unimaginable trials. This spiritual encounter became the foundation of her faith. It was not a cultural inheritance but a deeply personal relationship with God that offered my mother strength and gratitude amid the horrors of refugee life. Even in the camps, where clean water and nutritious food were scarce—and illnesses were rampant—she remained hopeful. And then, from across the world came a miracle.

The Role of Faith in Building a New Life

Thousands of miles away from Cambodia, in the small town of Berne, Indiana, two women in the First Mennonite Church congregation watched the news as awful wartime images and stories of refugees and "boat people" played out on the television in their living rooms. So many of us see images of crises, and we feel helpless to do anything. Yet these two women resolved that they were going to do something—they would save a family. They approached their pastor and asked if their church could sponsor a refugee family, and he agreed.

But this was no small undertaking. Sponsoring is not as simple as bringing a family to US shores. This church was, in essence, taking on the sacred responsibility of the lives of my family members in this new world. My family came in three groups over about eighteen months. At the church, meanwhile, there was a main committee dedicated to preparing to welcome these strangers into their midst. The details were assigned to smaller subcommittees. So many practicalities needed to be worked out. The church created committees for housing, transportation, healthcare, grocery shopping, clothing, language lessons, school enrollment, tutoring, finance lessons, and—importantly—employment.

My mom talks about the efforts of the church and the newness of this world:

> That's how we grew up [in Cambodia]. As you go to the market and buy everything daily.
>
> I grow up, I never have a bank, never have a bank. All we have family; all we have around the house. And so I don't know; I never understand about the banking thing until I came here, and mean, even though I lived here a few years, I still don't understand the bank. But we understand that we have a saving account we put in a bank. Sure, we do have that. … And later on, when we talked about school, we went to school in Fort Wayne. And then later on, the people from the church, Mennonite Church, have somebody that … she taught us. I think we gone to her house almost every night. So five night a week. Bless her heart. She usually taught in the morning. I love that. Those people. So we learned a lot from her. And then I went from home to home like schooling.

Initially, the congregation had our family live across the street from the church itself in a house the church had bought a few months prior. Congregants would drop by to try to make my family members feel more welcome, knowing they must have been scared and feeling overwhelmed. My family members would serve their visitors tea—but language was, of course, a stumbling block. The congregation, meanwhile, worried about my family's spiritual life, not just the ins and outs of making a life here. This was long before we ever, as a society, talked about mental health, but I am sure the pastor and others were concerned that my family was lonely, isolated—and homesick. Not for the Cambodia they left, but for the Cambodia of before the horrors.

At a Mennonite seminary, there was a man named David Chiu (mentioned briefly in chapter 3), a native of Hong Kong, who spoke both Cantonese and English. The church thought that maybe David could help. He would travel about an hour to our church on Sundays to be in a sound booth, and the church purchased headphones. David would translate as the service was going on. Now, Chinese is not Cambodian, but my family could understand snatches and words here and there—and both my parents are of Chinese descent. What an incredible testament to welcoming my family. The church even had an article written in the local paper asking for tutors from the wider community of Berne.

Tutors needed for Taing family

Volunteers from the community are being sought to tutor English to members of the Cambodian family living in Berne.

"Anyone in the community is welcome to volunteer," said Mrs. Steve (Mary Beth) Huser, who, with her husband, helps to coordinate the family's education. "Volunteers should be willing to spend an hour a week or more tutoring.

"But," she added, "we know people have vacations and summer plans. Volunteers don't have to be here every week."

Each volunteer will follow a textbook or plans prepared by a supervisor. No teaching experience is necessary, and no age requirements have been set for tutors.

The Taing family, sponsored by the First Mennonite Church of Berne, lives at the corner of Harrison and Franklin streets, Berne. The ten members of the family include the parents, five sons, two daughters, and a daughter-in-law. The children range in age from eight to 25 years old.

Volunteers are being sought especially for the children as three of them will be skipping a grade in school this coming fall.

"They can handle the math and other subjects, but they're really not ready in English," Mrs. Huser said.

The children are being advanced in school to get them closer to children their own age, she explained.

"If enough people volunteer, the parents will also be tutored," said Mrs. Huser.

Volunteers are welcome to state a preference as to which family member they would prefer working with — a girl or boy, younger or older family member.

Following are brief descriptions of each of family members:

Huy, the youngest, is eight years old. He will be going into second grade at South Adams this fall.

Chhit, is a 13-year-old boy, skipping from third grade this year into fifth grade this fall.

Lack is 15 years old. He will also be skipping a grade this fall, moving up from fifth grade to seventh grade at South Adams.

Poch is a first grader this year. She is 11 years old and plans have been made for her to advance to third grade this fall.

Ky, a daughter-in-law, and Sok are both 21 years old. They will not be employed this summer, so will be available with the children for tutoring during the day or evening.

Ngov, 19, works at Economy printing during the day. He will be available for tutoring in the evenings.

Ty, the oldest son and husband to Ky, is 25 years old. He is working under a CETA program and also does some studying in Decatur. But, he too would like to be tutored and would be available in the evenings.

The parents, commonly referred to by community members as Papa and Mama rather than by their names, Mong Kheang and Yin Vuon, both work during the day at Economy Printing.

Tutoring will begin the week of June 9. Anyone interested in helping the Taing family expand their knowledge of English may contact Mr. and Mrs. Steve Huser at 589-2024 to volunteer.

The tutoring ad placed in the Berne Witness newspaper.

For my parents, this was not simply a religious affiliation; it was a lifeline. The church not only brought them to the United States but also helped them find jobs, navigate societal norms, and foster meaningful relationships. This relationship with the church shaped their perspective on giving, service, and faith. Looking back, I see how these values permeated every aspect of my upbringing, from the lessons my parents taught us to Sunday School to the actions they modeled.

Gratitude and Faith

My parents' faith was inseparable from their gratitude for *life.* They really had two choices: They could be bitter about their experiences, or they could be grateful and look at life through that lens of appreciation. Again, long before people used terms such as *reframing negative experiences*, my parents were the original determined optimists, refusing to look at their lives in a negative way. My father often expressed gratitude for the opportunity to provide for his family, even if it meant never taking a day off. This ethos of gratitude and faith continues to inspire me.

For some people, I think God is a bit like Santa Claus. "Please bring me this or help me with that"—a list of wants. Their relationship with God is about what he can do for them, not one of discerning what he wants from us. Gratitude switches that view of God to an appreciation for all we have. My parents' experiences taught them never to take anything for granted. Whether it was a simple meal, a roof over their heads, or the chance to work, they saw every opportunity as a divine blessing.

These lessons have profoundly shaped my own values and priorities. They instilled in me a drive to succeed not for personal gain but to create positive change. My parents' sacrifices and their gratitude for even the smallest blessings became the foundation of my worldview and the legacy I now pass on to my children.

Faith Across Generations

As my parents have aged and become grandparents, their expressions of love have evolved. While they were not verbally affectionate with me as a child, they showed it through their protective natures.

However, they openly express love and affection for my children. It is beautiful to witness them hugging my daughters, telling them they love them, and even advising me to be more lenient as a parent. These moments are a testament to their growth, resilience, and enduring commitment to family. It makes my heart so happy to see them now getting to enjoy life a little (though my father just cannot be still—he still likes being busy).

The faith that carried my parents through their darkest days continues to guide me. It provides me with peace during challenges, strength to persevere, and gratitude for every moment of life. This faith, rooted in their journey of survival and grace, has rippled through my family's generations, shaping how I lead, live, and raise my children. Through their example, I have come to see faith not just as a religious practice but as a profound way of being—a source of hope, resilience, and compassion that defines who I am today.

My mother once told me that when I eventually went off to college, God would be watching me, and I should follow that straight path, not the crooked one. But I never looked at it that way. I found a church to go to when I was in college because, for me, a Sunday without attending church just felt as if something was missing. I suppose many teens envision that when they go off to college, they are going to have their freedom. And I did too. (If my parents weren't going to read this, I might say more!) But even with that freedom, I also maintained that tie to faith. Because of that, I always knew my God was with me.

In fact, when I went to college, I was excited (like many college freshmen) to have freedom and to not be under the watchful eyes of my parents—to meet new people and to have new experiences. Still, it wasn't until after college, when I was in dental school, that I was around other Asian students for the first time—and after living in

Indiana, in a town where the only Asians were people I was related to, this was exciting to me. But I discovered that, to some, I wasn't the "right" kind of Asian or wasn't Asian enough. So, I concentrated on my relationship with my best friend and those closest to me and, later, my boyfriend (now husband). I focused on my studies. But I don't think I felt lonely—because I had that personal relationship with God. I see my life's journey as part of something bigger. I feel like I see God's hand in every part of where life has taken me. And I am grateful for that.

I remember, as a child and young woman, there was such an emphasis placed on going to church every week. My mother always said, "Well, if you have time to go out and have fun, you have time to go to church." In other words, if you stay up late at night on Saturday night because you want to do whatever, you still have to go to church the next day no matter what.

Guess what? I have heard those exact same words leave my mouth to my own daughters! We become our parents a little (sometimes a lot). I say to my daughters now, "If we have friends over and you have time to stay up late and have fun with your friends, you still have to go to church on Sunday."

There is a reason the subtitle of this book includes the words "the power of showing up every day." Yes, my parents showed me this lesson by showing up at the donut shop every day, but also by their consistency of faith, showing up at church, volunteering, and showing up for the people in their lives who needed them.

My mom would never say anything negative about Buddhism when we would visit our relatives who were still practicing, but even with our Cambodian culture, we did not have Buddha statues in our home. My mom would say that their beliefs were fine for them, but for us, we worshipped a Christian God.

I remember when I left for college, my aunt gave me a Bible verse book, one of those small, pocket-size books that's easy to take along anywhere with you. I leaned on Jeremiah 29:11: "'For I know the plans I have for you,' declares the LORD, 'plans to prosper you and not to harm you, plans to give you hope and a future.'"

Ultimately, my faith is a set of guiding principles for me. I am grateful that I had a foundation that has shaped me into the person I am today, both personally and professionally. While I have seen family members with different views on faith and different principles, I feel a personal connection to the church that welcomed us when we first came to the United States.

Faith and Leadership

My faith doesn't end when I leave church on Sunday or when I leave my house in the morning. Like all people of faith—no matter their faith—it is something I carry with me all the time. And that includes the workplace.

I know that in today's modern world, people are often uncomfortable talking about faith—*especially in the workplace.* However, faith is a part of my leadership style. No, that does not mean I try to teach people religion or try to convert them—but faith informs my decisions as a leader. I will discuss leading with empathy in chapter 7, but it would not be authentic of me to share my own faith journey and my parents' if I left out this important element. The fact is, faith can be a set of guiding principles, regardless of which religion or practice you subscribe to, just as it is for my Buddhist family members. Faith helps clarify your principles around how you treat people. But for me, faith is all this and more—the thread of the church runs through my life, including in business.

Especially now that I'm a business owner, the verse that inspires me is Luke 12:48: "… unto whomsoever much is given, of him shall be much required: and to whom men have committed much, of him they will ask the more."

I was blessed with a family that valued education and shaped me to be a hard worker. I was given talents (something I will also discuss in the next chapter). I have achieved many of my dreams—and am still going strong. I have been able to give back. That is what the verse means to me as a leader. The blessings I have been given mean that I have a responsibility to do my best for—frankly—pretty much anyone I come in contact with, but I feel a special responsibility for my staff.

My faith guides my approach to leadership and creating a positive work environment. I strive to create a team that respects and cares for one another. I choose to lead by focusing on people's strengths rather than their weaknesses (something I will discuss in the next chapter).

It's incredibly important to me to positively impact those around me by integrating my faith into how I live out my beliefs. This practice involves balancing professionalism with following my personal values. I have a zero-tolerance policy for gossip, drama, and negativity in our office. While that is just smart culture in a professional environment (and something I'll also cover in more depth in a later chapter), it also aligns with my belief system and how I want to treat people—and how I want them to treat each other and our patients.

The workplace can sometimes present ethical dilemmas, in which you have to figure out how to not only resolve conflict but also ensure peace and harmony afterward. As a Christian, I have to have integrity, even when it's not easy. For instance, refusing to compromise on honesty in financial matters or prioritizing fair treatment of others reminds me of Proverbs 11:3, which says, "The integrity of the upright guides them," and also of Matthew 5:9, which states, "Blessed are the peacemakers, for they will be called children of God." Seeking solutions that honor both truth and relationships sets an example for others—and is how I want my staff to approach the natural and unavoidable conflicts that inevitably come up in the workplace.

Peacemaking fosters collaboration, practicing gratitude cultivates optimism, and remaining adaptable under pressure creates an agile work environment. Bringing faith into the workplace isn't about overt religious displays but about consistently reflecting God's love to others. Simple acts of kindness, such as celebrating coworkers' successes or supporting team members during stress, can create an atmosphere where others feel valued.

Helping

In the following picture of my family from a yellowed newspaper story, you can see that every person in that picture was in this new country, alive and safe, because two women over 8,700 miles away—strangers to my family—wanted to *help*.

WEDNESDAY, NOVEMBER 12, 1980 DECATUR DAILY DEMOCRAT, DECATUR, INDIANA

All but three of the family.

(Photo by June Grove)

Teaching Berne's new citizens the English language.

They lived a life that had no hope

by June Grove

First of a series on the Taing family, a group of 27 Cambodians who escaped Communist rule in their country and came to the United States to establish a home through the efforts of the First Mennonite Church in Berne.

William Golding, in his book, "Lord of the Flies," presents the hypothesis that man, if given the circumstances to be either good or evil, will choose the latter. Given enough time, evil will ultimately snuff out good in a confrontation that carries as its underlying theme, "Man's inhumanity to man."

As Americans, living in the atmosphere of a small town, we read of atrocities committed in Vietnam, Cambodia, Africa — and we pause, momentarily, to reflect. But we can't really comprehend the horror of it all — really FEEL what it would be like to be subject to an oppressor void of compassion.

Not so with the Taing family, which has within the last year escaped from Cambodia to be relocated in Berne, Indiana.

They KNOW what it's like to be starved, beaten, or shot.

When they see in magazines pictures of Communist guards keeping armed watch on Cambodian workers as they toil in the fields, they know that the picture shows the truth.

They KNOW the Communists. They KNOW the terror. They KNOW bone weary fatigue — for not long ago, the Taings and their relatives were among the thousands of Cambodians who were subjected to that kind of tyranny.

Actually, the Taings aren't Cambodian at all. They are Chinese, but long ago, their parents made the long trek from China to Battambang, Cambodia, where they started to build a life for themselves. The eight children, among them 26-year-old Ty Taing and 20-year-old Ngov Taing, were brought up on Cambodian soil.

Their father, Mong Taing, became a taxi driver, and he and wife Yin Vuon became wholesale dealers in clothing.

The Taings prospered through the years, accumulating some possessions, some gold, and three properties. Then in the mid 1970s the Communists came.

Nothing would ever be the same.

The Taings, their relatives, neighbors, and friends were put into work groups. Even pregnant women had to work in the fields right up to the time of delivery, and after one month, they were expected to go back to the fields again.

Babies were taken care of by old grandmothers, who weren't able to work. If the grandmother didn't want to take care of the baby, she would be unable to get any food, so no one refused.

Ty Taing told of his experiences. "I would have to get up at 3 a.m.," he began, "and then walk five miles to the field where I was to work all day. We would work till noon when we would get lunch."

That lunch consisted of rice and salt. That's all — and that was the only meal that Ty and the others would get all day. Even back in their house, they had no food unless they had money or gold or something that they could trade.

Luckily, Ty's mother had about 40 ounces of gold which they used to buy food. "If we hadn't had that," said Ty, "we would more than likely have died."

After the lunch of rice and salt, the Cambodians kept working until 7 p.m., when they would quit and then have to walk back home again.

But that didn't end their day. Not at all.

Outside each of the houses in which the workers stayed was a garden. But the garden didn't belong to the workers. It belonged to the Communists.

It wasn't the Communists who tended that garden, though. It was the workers who had toiled in the fields all day and then walked home.

"Usually I got done taking care of the garden and hoeing out the weeds about ten o'clock at night," said Ty.

He also said that if he had tried to take one carrot from that garden he would have been punished. What the Communists did with all the food reaped from the fields and the gardens, the Cambodians never knew. Some of them tried to find out but were unsuccessful. All they knew was that they didn't get any of it.

This kind of life went on day after day, seven days a week. The Cambodians and the Taing family grew thin. Most people developed stomach problems.

To supplement their meager diet, they made soup with the stalks of banana trees with tree roots as their vegetables. The Communists gave the people three glasses of rice for 30 people for one meal — which didn't go very far. "We would put in a lot of water to make it last longer," said Ty.

The price of commodities was exorbitant. For instance, for a bottle of aspirin, the Cambodians would have to pay a watch or perhaps a small diamond.

No one would take paper money. It had to be gold or diamonds or something that would be good on any market. "If you didn't have any of these things and someone got sick, then you couldn't buy medicine," explained Ty, "and you would just die."

Children old enough to work were not sent to the same fields as were their parents, and if they cried they were beaten up or abused in other manners. For instance, Ty said that he heard about one child who cried and one of the Communists threw a pumpkin at him, breaking it over his head.

Sometimes young single people were sent away into the forests to start a village. But the problem was — these people were given no tools or any food, and they were expected to clear the forest, build houses, and plant gardens with only their hands.

"Usually, they didn't return," said Ty.

So what the workers tried to do was to get married as soon as possible so they wouldn't be left to the fate of the single people.

"People would get married even if they didn't particularly like one another," Ty said.

Because of the heavy work schedule, a man and his wife didn't see one another for more than about three times a month, anyway.

The people were not allowed to have any kind of religion. "We weren't allowed to believe in anything," Ty said. The Communists had destroyed all the churches and the temples.

Then they told the people, "Religion won't save you. Only work will save you."

The intellectuals — the ones who might be able to organize the Cambodians to resist the Communists — were killed right away.

For four years, the Taing family worked in the fields and lived the life that had no hope. Then the Vietnamese soldiers arrived. After that, no one worked on the farms anymore and each family had to get along as best they could.

There seemed to be nothing. The Taings decided to try and leave Cambodia to head for a refugee camp in Thailand.

There are 27 Taings (All relatives are included in the count.) who have come from Thailand to the United States.

The first group of ten to arrive came in September, 1979, and it was this group which included Mon Taing, Yin Vuan (Mong's wife), and Ty and Ngov Taing.

They were brought to Berne through the efforts of the First Mennonite Church of Berne under the auspices of the Mennonite Central Committee.

After the Taings were established in Berne, they thought about their other relatives — the rest of their family — who were still in Cambodia, and they longed to have them come to America, too.

Since the first family of Taings was already established in America, it was easier to get the others here, too, if they could be located. This is where Eldon Claasson, a registered nurse from Berne, came in.

He went over to the camps in Thailand where the refugee Cambodians had fled, and through much effort, finally located more of the family.

In September, 1980, eleven more of the Taing family arrived in Berne, and just a couple of weeks ago, Yin Fong, sister to Yin Vuon, and six more of the family, including the grandmother, arrived in Berne.

To be continued.

November 12, 1980. Photo by June Grove for the Decatur Daily Democrat. *Top row (left to right): Ngov Taing, Kim Hin Pung, Kan Sang Chau, Fou Kheng Chau, Yi Chau, Ty Taing, Ky Taing, Lack Taing, Ty Chau, Cheung Chau, and Giu Chau. Second row: Hean Heong Chau (my great-grandmother), Yin Vuon (my grandmother), Mong Kheng Taing (my grandfather), and Gee Chau. Third row: Mung Chau, Yin Fong, and Wan Chau. Fourth row (bottom): Cheung Chau, Ty Chau, Mong Chau, Moi Taing (holding Mey Chau), Michael Taing, and Lee Taing.*

After years of growing up in the church, when it was my time to step up and help, I did. I shared earlier in the book about the mission trip I took that set me on my path toward dentistry and working with kids. That mission trip instilled in me a dedication to helping—something I continue to do to this day.

I often think about my mom's initial plea to God for salvation. It was the beginning of a journey that has led our family to a profound sense of gratitude, resilience, and a commitment to serving others. This unwavering faith continues to define my character and my commitment to making a positive impact on the world.

Faith Through Life's Trials

As I wrote earlier, my parents were able to locate my maternal grandmother with the help of a missionary associated with their church. But there were still more trials ahead of them. When they returned to the United States, my father had to live separately from us in order to work. In his words:

> Mom, we find her. We got children, do some sponsor papers to bring over here. I got my business sold too, so I don't have no job after I sold my business. So I go, I work in Glenn, Michigan. My wife stay in Indiana, and I go by myself to work. I come home sometimes on the weekend. You got do right. So I worked for about a year, and then they got a business for sale right now in Fort Wayne, the one I own right now for sale. And the owner, he said, "You want to buy my business? I ready to sell now."
>
> I said, "How much?"
>
> He [told me the price].

> I said, "Well, I don't have [that]," but I [told him what I had].
>
> He said, "OK, I take it, but you make a payment for me."
>
> So I bought the business from him; I owe a year and a half. I tried to approach the building right now, the Tom Donut. I tried to buy the building because I don't want to rent because I pay rent and then all the money go to the rent.
>
> So I want to own the building. So [the owner], his name is John. He said, "You want to buy my building?"
>
> I said, "Yeah, how much you want to sell?"
>
> Once again, my dad did not have the full amount, but he offered to make payments:
>
> He said, "How many years you want?"
>
> I said, "Well, eight to nine years. I don't want to owe people too long."
>
> But I try to work and pay for it. So I paid all the loan business and the building.
>
> I paid for nine year. Then we bring [my mom's] family here and tell kids, go to school. I tell all my kids; I say, "You wait, make sure you go to school. You want to become somebody."

I know faith and determination got my parents through those years. My husband and I had a long-distance relationship for a while too, and I think I knew I could handle that because I understood sacrificing for long-term goals and because I also had my faith to lean on—both invaluable gifts from my parents. They worked hard to instill these values in me because they believed in me. They knew my own strengths before I did. And especially as I started to develop my own leadership style, I found yet another gift from them in their support.

ptember 9, 1980 Vol. 3 No. 19
aing Relatives Arrive
Refugees Bri
Free at last!
Taing relatives begi

CHAPTER 5

Leaning into Innate Talents

Your talent is God's gift to you. What you do with it is your gift back to God.

~ LEO BUSCAGLIA

Growing up, I never considered myself a natural leader. I wasn't the type to run for student council or to eagerly volunteer to speak in front of a crowd. Actually, I suppose I did not think too much about leadership at all. I don't think many kids do. Instead, I was studious, driven to succeed academically because my parents instilled in me a deep appreciation for education. They sacrificed so much to ensure I had opportunities they never did, and they encouraged me to pursue a career in which I could help people. But leading a team, inspiring others? That felt like a different skill set altogether. I had this image in my head of a leader as someone very authoritative, very bottom line, and without a lot of empathy. Leaders even seemed a little bit scary.

And, as I said, I am naturally introverted—even to this day. That may seem odd since I own and run my own practice and am the public face of Warsaw Orthodontics; however, I can push through my natural shyness. I have created a practice that is joyful—I made it my own natural habitat. And, of course, kids and I connect on a whole other level. I love making them laugh, helping them get over any nervousness, or just making them feel special and important.

It wasn't until I was in my orthodontic residency that I realized I needed to develop my leadership skills. I mentioned earlier that one afternoon, while still in my residency, I had been in a hurry and feeling impatient, so I had rushed someone who was just learning how to take x-rays. When the faculty member supervising me had pulled me aside, they had made it clear that my job would not only be fixing teeth but also communicating in a healthy way with those around me. That had been a wake-up call. I realized I couldn't just be good at the technical aspects of my profession; I needed to learn how to lead a team effectively.

That's when I discovered leadership books. I'd get ready in the morning and listen to audiobooks to figure out where to even start. I wanted to figure out how I was going to communicate with my future team. I took a little from each book—but no leadership model fully spoke to who I was and what my values were. Until I found *StrengthsFinder 2.0.*

Discovering My Strengths

As I immersed myself in the world of leadership literature and explored different leadership philosophies, I came across the book *StrengthsFinder 2.0*, released by Gallup, which emphasizes building a *strengths-based team* and provides an assessment that promises to teach readers about their strengths. Curious, I decided to take the assessment. (What did I have to lose?) The assessment covers thirty-four themes and only takes about thirty minutes to do. You're presented with a series of statements that comprise two extremes. For example, "I am a sensitive person" might be at one end of the scale. On the opposite end would be "I am a logical person." Another might be, "Starting conversations is an effort for me" (for us introverts) versus "I get a rush from striking up a conversation with a stranger" (for all you extroverts).[2]

And if neither of those extremes feels quite right for you—because these are intentionally not simple yes or no questions—you can mark yourself along a scale between the two statements. For example, if you feel you could be sensitive or logical depending on the situation, you could mark a neutral position along the scale.

There are thirty-four CliftonStrengths between four domains (Executing, Influencing, Relationship Building, and Strategic Thinking). Most people don't have a perfect balance of strengths across all four areas. Whichever categories the bulk of your strengths fall under, you know that those are some of your top skills. When I got my own results, I was shocked at how accurately it assessed me—Harmony was my top strength, followed by Consistency, Futuristic, Empathy, and Developer. When I read my report, I found myself nodding my head.

My natural inclination is to avoid conflict, which is the basement of the strength Harmony. In other words, harmony is a great strength, but at its weakest position, avoiding conflict (which often means not communicating) is a problem. For a long time for me, that meant not

2 "Use the CliftonStrengths Assessment to Discover & Develop Your Greatest Talents," Gallup, https://www.gallup.com/cliftonstrengths/en/253676/how-cliftonstrengths-works.aspx.

addressing the little things that bothered me or my team members, hoping those things would just go away. (Spoiler alert: They don't.) Someone who avoids conflict might also, for example, model the behaviors they want (such as not gossiping or being patient) and hope that the team learns it by observation—or osmosis.

It does not work that way either.

My desire for harmony also meant that sometimes I would say something with the intention to help, anything to try to restore harmony. But it would instead come off wrong because I hadn't processed my thoughts thoroughly or communicated them well. I was reacting instead of responding, and when you are the boss or the leader, your words carry a heavier weight.

My Communication strength allows me to express my vision clearly and empathetically. I tend to overcommunicate, but it's because I've seen what happens when people are left to fill in the gaps and make up their own stories. I've learned that a lack of communication creates a breeding ground for negativity. I tell my staff the wise words of author and business consultant Jon Gordon: *Where there's a void in communication, negativity will fill it.*[3] This concept has really transformed how we address issues at our practice. We do not let things fester, which would be like inviting infection into an open wound.

Empathy is another one of my key strengths. It's not just about feeling for someone; it's about trying to understand their experiences and perspectives—something that's incredibly important to me given the challenges my family has faced. When I was talking with my mom about this book, she told me a story about how people would come into the donut shop and mock my parents' English or their very "Asianness":

3 Jon Gordon, "The 4 C's to Improve Your Relationships and Team," The Jon Gordon Companies, n.d., https://jongordon.com/positivetip/4cs.html.

> Fort Wayne, where I live, I don't see a lot of Cambodian. They have somewhere scatter around Fort Wayne. Farther, from school maybe. And [Emily's] the only black-head girl. True. Joan and Emily is, and a small school by my house here. Now I always tell Emily too, I said maybe somebody will making fun of her. We warning her about that. I know when she—we work in a donut shop in North Manchester, we don't understand "wing-ding-ding-dong" mean in a donut shop. People call him all kind of names. We don't know. We laugh along.

Now, as a mother, as a person of faith, I cannot understand the casual cruelty of prejudice. Where is the empathy for others? These experiences influenced how I see the world. Thus, for me, empathy is about creating a safe space where people feel seen, heard, and valued. I understand that my staff members are not just employees; they are individuals with their own lives and challenges. I want them to feel supported and cared for so they can bring their best selves to work every day.

Next, the strength of Consistency is, for me, about treating everyone fairly and equally. It means that I strive to set clear expectations and hold everyone to the same standards. I don't play favorites; I believe everyone deserves to be treated with respect and consideration. Consistency allows for a sense of reliability. It lets my team know that they can depend on me to address problems or concerns fairly.

Even as I was nodding along reading my results, at first, I didn't see how some of these could fit into a leadership style at all. I always thought that a leader should be direct, decisive, and maybe even a bit demanding, not someone who valued harmony and connection.

I soon realized, though, that these weren't weaknesses—they were my greatest assets if I learned to use them in the right ways.

Have you ever had the experience where you learn about something new, and then you start to notice it everywhere? You'd never had certain conversations before, but now the topic seems to come up all the time? Well, shortly after taking the CliftonStrengths assessment, I found out about an orthodontic meeting in which consultant Vicki Newell was presenting "How to Build a Strength-Based Team" based on the Gallup assessment. I considered it a bit of a sign, and so I decided to attend. After she had given her presentation, I approached her because I was interested in focusing on what people could do well instead of nitpicking on their shortcomings. It seemed to me that understanding the strengths of each member of my team—as well as my own strengths—could help take our practice to the next level. That initial conversation with Vicki led to a coaching relationship that has profoundly shaped my leadership style over the past ten years.

Why I Chose Strengths-Based Leadership

The idea behind the StrengthsFinder® assessment is to focus on what individuals do best and not what they don't do well. I had seen firsthand how a negative environment could bring down an entire team. I had also experienced that kind of environment in a previous job. Even once I had bought the practice, the culture did not change overnight. In my practice, I wanted to create a team of people who respected and cared for one another.

I hired Vicki because I did not want to constantly tell people what they were doing wrong. Everyone has had that boss or professor who criticized them until they lost their confidence. As someone who values harmony, that was not how I wanted to guide my team. Instead, I wanted to create a positive work environment where we all supported each other.

It was through my work with Vicki that I learned that harmony is not about avoiding conflict. Instead, it is about creating an environment where everyone feels heard and valued. It's about understanding different perspectives and finding common ground. *That's* what I wanted for my practice.

I also learned from Vicki something that we all know innately is true: Gossip never leads to anything good and can tear a group completely apart. Her philosophy was that when you focus on people's strengths, and not their weaknesses, you're able to cultivate a much more productive and enjoyable work experience, one that does not tolerate speaking about people behind their backs. And so that's what I sought to do in my workplace.

Not only did Vicki teach me that gossip isn't healthy in the workplace, but she also gave me the tools and taught me the leadership style I needed to ensure that gossip didn't happen. What I learned from her became foundational to my practice, not just for me but for my staff too. To me, it was amazing how things threaded together because this kind of leadership also fits my faith. Vicki taught me to develop my own leadership style, one that isn't about being the loudest or most demanding person in the room (which, frankly, no one's leadership style should be). It's about creating a culture where everyone feels empowered, valued, and respected. It's about encouraging open communication, understanding different perspectives, and finding ways to work together harmoniously. It's about recognizing that we are all interconnected and that each person's well-being is important.

Leaning into strengths-based leadership allowed me to similarly lean into the things that make me *me*—the things that make my practice a place that's safe and inviting for my staff and my patients. They're my faith, my desire to help others, my dedication. They're not forced or forceful. They're not judgmental or unkind. I get to lead, but I don't have to sacrifice aspects of myself to be a leader. The CliftonStrengths assessment and Vicki helped me see what my parents see in me. There were times when I doubted myself, when I didn't know what I didn't know, but my parents never stopped pushing and believing in me. As my mom said:

> [We] believe in her because she [has] drive. We can see that she want to work hard. And I knew that she's not going to like it when she worked with somebody partner or something like that. And she want [to] make her own decision. That's what I'm thinking. Because that will ... she want to make her own decision, and she don't want to listen. She don't want to listen to me. Before I knew that. And so, I thought ... we thought that she should own her own business, and I'm support of that. And she have a number for me. She was scared. She was scared when she's done with dental school too; when she go to become an orthodontist, she was crying because she owe people money so much. She keep paying the interest only. So a lot of money still all there. But I keep telling her it's OK. I mean we owe people money, and we take long time to pay off too ... we take all three different people to pay off the loan and stuff like that.

Knowing my parents believed in me gave me a little extra courage to tackle these leadership issues head-on. And, while I was writing this book, I had my parents take the StrengthsFinder assessment too. My mom's strengths were Consistency, Connectedness, Learner, Harmony, and Responsibility. My dad got Consistency, Relator, Deliberative,

Positivity, and Significance. I already knew I owed much of my perspective and personality to them, but it was fascinating to have that validated in this way—I could see what I got from each of them!

Within my business, after a lot of practice and implementation, I have found that this strengths-based approach not only makes my team happier and more engaged; it also makes them more productive and creative. Since we're not busy worrying about office gossip or drama, we can focus on what matters most: our patients. And, of course, supporting each other. I don't just like to *think* that coming to our practice is a happy, positive experience—I know it is, because I see it in my patients, and their parents love to tell me it is from time to time too.

Putting My Strengths into Practice

Over the years, I've learned to apply my strengths in various situations. I've developed practical ways to create a harmonious, consistent environment; communicate effectively; and lead with empathy. Here are some examples of how these strengths play out in my practice:

ADDRESSING CONFLICT AND BUILDING CONSENSUS

When conflict arises, my inclination to avoid it initially kicks in. I'm not going to lie—conflict used to make me physically uncomfortable; my heart rate would increase, I'd feel hot, and even my voice would change. In fact, I used to write out what I wanted to say so that I wouldn't forget things and would feel more confident about addressing the issue at hand. Over time, I've learned to pause, breathe, and assess the situation objectively. Instead of trying to assign blame, I am solution-focused. I try to bring people together to come to an agreement. I focus on the common goal and on what's best for our patients. Then I use my communication skills to clearly explain everyone's roles and expectations. Conflict in the workplace is something that must be addressed directly and productively. Avoiding conflict is never beneficial in the long run. I've had to learn how to use my Harmony strength in a constructive way, looking to find consensus rather than just trying to avoid disagreements. When everyone keeps the mission in mind—no matter what business you are in—it is easier to find common ground.

ZERO TOLERANCE FOR NEGATIVITY

As I said, I have a zero-tolerance policy for gossip, drama, and negativity in my office because I know firsthand how damaging they can be. I have witnessed how negativity can bring down an entire team, so it is something I actively work to avoid. I strive to create an environment where my staff members respect and care for one another, and that starts with me setting the tone for the day. My zero-tolerance policy also extends to how my team solves conflict. When someone shares a complaint or has an issue with another person on the team, I expect them to go to that person directly. But that is not always easy for people (after all, I used to have to write down my thoughts—which I still do now!). So, what does conflict resolution look like in practice? If someone on my staff is not comfortable being direct, I encourage them to have a "courageous conversation," which we practice together. Unsurprisingly, because I want a harmonious workplace, I have many staff members who also value harmony, and so it *does* take courage for most of us. From there, if necessary, I will be part of that conversation with everyone so that we all get on the same page. Whenever we have these kinds of conversations, I'm always aiming to share the same tools I've learned so they can build on their own strengths and communicate effectively.

RECOGNIZING CORE VALUES

I aim to create a culture of open communication, where everyone overcommunicates to avoid misunderstandings. As I said, I encourage my staff members to talk directly to each other to resolve issues instead of complaining to me or others. When a conflict or breakdown in communication does occur, I try to bring the team back to its core values and how we can better serve our patients and each other.

DELEGATION AND TRUST

As that straight-A student with a strict background and always wanting to do my best, it would be easy for me to take on everything. One big lesson I had to learn was that I am human and just one person (imagine that!). I had to learn to delegate more, to trust my team, and to not micromanage. I have found that clearly expressing my expectations is important. I have also learned that, as a leader, I need to convey my vision and encourage my staff to not just go along with it but to be excited about it.

FINDING COMMON GROUND

My team can always find something to agree on. Even if the only common ground is, "We want our patients to feel happy and cared for from the moment they walk in the door and to feel good about their orthodontic treatment"—this is something every person on my staff can agree on. I once had a situation where a patient's brackets hadn't been cleaned properly, and instead of placing blame, I redirected everyone's focus to our core value of service to get back on track. In that way, conflict becomes an opportunity to find common ground—to mentor and guide. While I do not like conflict, I recognize that it is part of life, marriage, business, and family, and I try to handle each conflict situation with grace and communication.

SET CLEAR EXPECTATIONS

Some things that seem obvious to one person may not be to another. I think that my team is finally in a place where everyone understands the expectations of my leadership, which has allowed my practice to grow and improve. I strive to make sure that my workplace is a place where all staff members can thrive and grow in their own careers—and that is only possible if expectations and goals are clear to us all.

MANAGING DISAGREEMENTS

I also discovered through coaching that I had to learn to regulate my body and breathe through situations when I felt uncomfortable so that I could remain calm and clear. I would easily get flustered. Through coaching, I learned to see disagreements not as personal attacks but as opportunities to improve our systems and processes. If we can all come to an agreement, it will allow us to serve our patients and each other better.

GROWING TOGETHER

As I've said, I make it a point to develop our team members as individuals and as a group. Our staff even has a book club together. We pick books that have to do with leadership and how to communicate, so that's another way that our office focuses on becoming a healthy team. One of the books we read was Brené Brown's *Dare to Lead*, which we took two years to get through because it was so chock-full of excellent advice and concepts. Through these books, my staff has realized that there are always better ways to communicate and that we are all working toward the same goals. We've also read *The Energy Bus* by Jon Gordon, which is about creating a positive team culture, and *Lessons from the Mouse* by Dennis Snow to learn about excellent customer service.

USING CONSISTENCY

My commitment to fairness, even when I am tired and exhausted, is a huge part of how I lead. I have systems in place for almost every task. For example, when I first bought the practice, all the charts were paper, and it was chaos. I needed to implement new systems, including electronic charting. This was a difficult task, and when I began to implement it, one of the former employees told me that I couldn't just come in and change everything. But having systems, even for how we implement systems, allows for consistency and efficiency. I have also had people leave the practice because they wanted special treatment—but consistency demands I not do so in order to not build resentment.

OVERCOMMUNICATING

I believe in overcommunication because, as I have said, when there's a void in communication, negativity will fill it. This philosophy is the backbone of my business. I am clear with my vision, and when we have goals, I make sure to share them with the entire team. But, for leaders, it is also important to share the reasons why we do what we do. When everyone has a better understanding of the purpose behind what they're doing, it is easier to do our jobs. And it makes team buy-in of our core values easier—we all understand why we are doing things the way we are.

Through it all, the biggest surprise that I've had as a leader, especially since utilizing StrengthsFinder, is that leading doesn't mean trying to be someone I'm not. I thought that leaders had to be authoritative, demanding, and maybe a little intimidating. I have instead learned that I can lead effectively using my natural strengths. It's much easier to lead when you understand your strengths rather than trying to squeeze into a mold that isn't a good fit.

The other thing that has been the biggest surprise for me is that managing people is hard! For someone who values harmony, it is not natural for me to have difficult conversations. However, I realized that by avoiding those situations, I was creating a culture of resentment. So, through coaching and practice, I've become more comfortable having those courageous conversations with my team, and by communicating my needs and expectations clearly, I've created a culture of honesty and accountability.

Moving Forward

My journey as a leader has been one of self-discovery and growth. I have embraced my natural strengths and learned to use them effectively. I've built a team that values communication, respect, and collaboration, and we all serve our patients and each other to the best of our abilities.

The idea that you need to be a certain type of leader to succeed is simply untrue. The most effective leaders are those who are *authentic* and *genuine.* When we understand our strengths and learn how to use them wisely, it's not only better for our own well-being but also for our teams and our businesses. That's what I am trying to teach my daughters now. It's not about being the most talented or the most successful; it's about doing the best that we can to make the world a better place. I remind them, "You need to do your best," and "You have to learn so you can help people."

I am excited about the future of my practice, and I am committed to creating a place where we can all continue to grow. Because, in the end, that is what leadership is all about: helping each other be our best selves.

CHAPTER 6

Discovering Core Values

A quiet conscience makes one strong!

~ ANNE FRANK

Strengths-based leadership is important to me. It fits my mindset of how I want to treat people. But strengths are nothing if they are not applied. That aspect of leadership is really about core values—not just determining what your core values are, but *living* them each and every day. I wanted that not just for myself but for my team.

One of the gifts of being a first-generation daughter of hardworking immigrants is that, as a child and teen, I needed to accept that my family was different. We looked different from everyone else in our Midwest town. I was born here; I am American, but I had the blessing of knowing my family ate different foods (I am not the only first-generation kid who had different lunches from their friends at school), had different traditions, and had a specific set of core values that I knew I had to live up to.

When you are different, you have two choices. You can try to conform and be like everybody else, which is an understandable choice—adolescence is full of so much peer pressure. And I had my fair share of moments when I wanted to be like everyone else—I wanted to go to slumber parties, but I was the only girl whose parents would pick her up at nine o'clock and not let her stay the night. In hindsight, my adolescence often felt like a push-pull between my parents and me. I wanted to do the things my friends did—ordinary American experiences. But my parents were protective. They would always reiterate that although my friends' parents were letting them go out, *our* family was different—they were not like my friends' parents. Of course, now I understand. My parents *had* no ordinary adolescence. After what they had experienced, every fiber of their beings was very much about wanting to keep their children safe.

It was a simple fact: My parents were different; I was different. So, after a time, after maturing, I came to understand how beautiful being different was.

You can embrace being different.

In the times when I felt lonely in college and dental school, I turned to my faith and my own inner strength, both of which I had because of my parents. I learned to be OK with being a bit of an outsider. I didn't need to have tons of friends. (As my mother and father would remind me, it's better to have one good friend than many who might lead you off your path.) I was always more concerned with real friends, with quality relationships. I knew my own core values and worth, and I wasn't about to let fair-weather friends or anyone else guide me away from the path my family had fought hard for me to have simply because I was different.

Then, once I was leading my orthodontic practice, from a leadership perspective, I came to realize not only that being different is OK—more than OK even—but that everyone in a workplace benefits from having shared values, regardless of our other differences. Shared values keep us focused on what we want to achieve as a team. We can row the proverbial boat together in the same direction. So, I did an exercise with my team where we decided to come up with our shared core values—together.

Going through the exercise and discussion together was essential to our success. That kind of collaboration is the real secret to collective satisfaction and motivation. Top-down leadership where someone dictates, "It's my way or the highway," isn't helpful. I have seen many different kinds of orthodontists in practice, in school, etc., and I have never felt that the authoritarian approach works. When I saw people lead in that way, I knew I wanted to do the opposite. Instead, my team and I—and a giant whiteboard—pulled together the values that we would embody. This is actually a technique from the book *Traction* by Gino Wickman, and something we've found very valuable.

At the brainstorming session where we came up with our core values, we wrote down *a lot* of words and concepts that were meaningful to each of us. Once we had exhausted our ideas of words for our core values, we needed to settle on the ones that felt most like *us* and that would create the kind of workplace where we all wanted to be.

Core values reflect what is most important to an individual or group. They cannot just be words—they have to be lived. At the end of that day, the five core values of my practice and team—of me!—were and are:

1. Service
2. Positivity
3. Integrity
4. Team Player
5. Pride in Your Work

As I looked at the results on the whiteboard, I related to the five values and felt that they truly represented my own core principles. We may have come up with them all together, but I personally related to all of them—and because we'd done this exercise together, everyone else felt that way too. Of course, as I thought about each value, I saw more parallels with my parents.

Service

When I was young, I would spend time at the donut shop on weekends or after school with my parents. I did not realize it at the time, but both my dad and my mom would have their regular customers' orders memorized. It was seamless (which is probably why I did not realize it). They would watch customers approach the shop from the sidewalk, so when they saw one of their regulars walking over, my parents already knew what size coffee, how many sugars, and how much cream the customer would want. My dad would tell me, "Go get me a large coffee," or whatever the order was, before the customer even walked in the door. By the time the customer made it to the counter, their coffee was already ready and waiting for them at the cash register. Talk about service!

In fact, my parents were unfailingly polite to anyone who walked through the donut shop's door. If you have ever been in the service industry—a job in retail or at a restaurant—then you know that not every customer is easy to deal with. My parents did not read leadership books or go to business school. They just had a natural way with people—a kindness that translated to service. It was their nature to shrug off unpleasantness or even outright racism—and their commitment to service gave them a graciousness some did not deserve.

However, as a leader, I now understand that service is not a single industry. It's not only donut shops and cafés and grocery stores. Service is every encounter your company, business, or organization has with its own staff and with its customers, clients, or just those your business comes in contact with. Service is everything today. (And increasingly, service is not good, people are stressed, businesses are understaffed, etc.)

In our practice, we believe service has to start with each other, with our team. Supporting one another is at the center of what we do, which means our staff is "tight." We have to take care of and appreciate one another first so we can then provide great service to our patients. I want each and every one of us to consider our team and our patients as family. We ask ourselves, "How can we make our patients' experiences at our practice and in all their dealings with us"—whether that is appointment reminders, the visits themselves, scheduling, etc.—"seamless and efficient, as well as positive and caring? How can we provide the best service possible to our patients and their families?" As an orthodontist, service to patients and their families is at the heart of everything I do. This commitment stems from my upbringing and my parents' emphasis on helping others. I strive to create a practice where patients feel valued, supported, and cared for throughout their orthodontic journey. They are part of our practice's family, and I want them to feel that way. And as a doctor who works with young people, I've seen up close and personal how much kids have to deal with these days, from bullying, chaotic home lives, the pressures of social media, peer pressure, and so much more. I strive—and our practice strives—to make these kids laugh and smile, to build their confidence, and to make the visit to our practice the best part of their day!

Drawing from my own experience both as a patient and now as a provider, I've developed specific practices that embody our practice's commitment to service. When I think about what makes me feel valued as a human being, I implement those same principles in our practice. Each day, I try to channel the warm welcome my parents offered to every customer who entered their donut shop. Here's how that commitment to care and service takes shape in our practice:

- **Greeting patients warmly.** When anyone walks in the door, they should feel that we care. For some people, a visit to a dental, orthodontic, or medical office is anxiety-provoking. We want walking into our practice to feel *fun* and truly convey the way we feel about our patients.
- **Creating a comfortable and welcoming environment.** This isn't just for the patients and their families. I want my team to be excited to come to work, to feel they are welcome and cared for. I know that will make them more effective at their jobs. Happy employees, comfortable employees, welcomed employees—they convey that back to the people we serve.
- **Taking the time to listen to patients' (and team members') concerns to understand their goals.** Whether a young patient is worried something might hurt or an adult wants to understand the aligner process on their way to a straighter smile, when we take time to listen, we provide the right type of care. This commitment to listening also includes, once again, my team. When team members feel listened to, they are more likely, in turn, to be listeners and to demonstrate caring through that listening skill.
- **Ensuring patients feel that their journey through our office is smooth.** I'm a busy mom. My husband is a first responder. I own a thriving practice—in two locations. It takes a village, I say, with my girls. I am very grateful for my

> parents and in-laws, and I have had great nannies. I have an amazing team in my offices. All of this is to say that in the busy lives of modern families, a visit to the orthodontist should be the least of their worries. I understand the lives of car pools and after-school activities. Service means that visits should be smooth—and that communications about them should be clear.

Ultimately, I want to build relationships with my patients and their families, not just treat their teeth. I want to connect with the kids who come in—excited, nervous, or both—to get their braces, and I want their families to feel that their children are in trusted hands.

Always, I ask myself, *How can I and my staff best serve the people who put their trust in us?* My Christian faith deeply informs my commitment to serving others, as I view service as a tangible way to express my beliefs through action. I strive to cultivate a team and work environment characterized by respect and genuine care for one another. For me, faith isn't confined to Sundays but is a constant presence guiding my decisions daily.

A key aspect of this connection lies in the responsibility and gratitude I feel. Because I've been given so much, I believe that much is required of me, especially as it relates to my team and my patients. As written in Luke 12:48: "For unto whomsoever much is given, of him shall be much required."

Another aspect of service I am passionate about is my commitment to staying current in technological best practices. I will never forget the first months of running my practice and the struggle to make the changes necessary to bring it into a more modern, digital age. It was not easy getting an established staff that was used to paper processes to trust that the changes would make the practice better. Change for the sake of change just invites chaos. Change aligned with goals and a commitment to service is positive change. It might be temporarily uncomfortable, but it will get you where you want to be.

Providing high-quality orthodontic care is essential to serving my patients. I remain committed to staying up to date with the latest advancements in orthodontics and investing in technology that allows us to deliver the most effective and efficient treatment. For example, my practice uses DentalMonitoring, an AI platform that allows patients to scan their teeth with their smartphone. I check in every day and provide feedback on the platform. What could be more convenient? *The gift of time* is a service, so saving someone an office visit and being able to do this weekly check if need be is an amazing advancement.

I also believe that patient education is a crucial aspect of service. I take the time to explain treatment options, discuss the benefits and risks of each approach, and answer any questions that patients or their families may have. I want my patients to feel empowered to make informed decisions about their oral health. I also make sure I speak to young patients in an age-appropriate and inclusive way so that they feel like they're a part of their own oral health and orthodontic journey.

Of course, I strive to create a culture of empathy within my practice. I encourage everyone on my team to put themselves in our patients' shoes and to treat everyone with compassion and understanding. As a woman and a mother, I also find that I can connect with my patients, especially the moms, on a deeper level. I understand the challenges that families face, and I work to accommodate their needs and schedules. As I've said, understanding the stresses of the modern family on the go means I can relate to time constraints and parental stress, and that guides me as I try to make improvements to enhance our practice's service even more.

My commitment to service also extends beyond the walls of my practice. As someone who benefited from the generosity of others when my family first came to the United States, I feel a strong sense of responsibility to give back to my community. As a child, I was aware that the church that sponsored my family not only saved them from the uncertainty of a refugee camp but also helped with all of their needs, from groceries to tutoring. Consequently, from my first mission trip to volunteering with my current church, I feel a strong sense of responsibility toward others—probably going back as far as that conversation with my dad in the car when he told me to become a doctor: "That way, you will be able to help people."

A commitment to service should be ongoing. As I mentioned, there was initially some pushback when I wanted to update the practice I purchased. This was years ago, and it took time to pull together the *right* team, to build trust within that team, and to train and develop myself and my people so that our service and warmth are now hallmarks of our practice. Service needs to be woven into the fabric of any business.

Ultimately, service to our patients and their families is about more than just straightening teeth. It's about making a positive impact on their lives. By providing compassionate care, empowering patients through education, and giving back to my community, I strive to create a practice that truly makes a difference. I make it a point to remind the team at every huddle that "Our number one core value is service—*to our patients, each other, and our community.*"

Positivity

My father is one of those people who will talk to anyone—again, strangers are just friends he has not met yet. We've also all heard the expression about someone being so kind that they would give someone else the shirt off their own back. Yes, cliché—but these are two traits my father embodies. Both he and my mother exude positivity.

Anyone who has endured war and hardship has a choice—to become bitter or to reject that bitterness and face the future with gratitude. My parents chose the latter and set such a wonderful example for my siblings and me.

When positivity made the final five on the whiteboard among our shared core values, I thought of my dad right away. When people in the donut shop would ask my father, "How are you doing today?" he would always reply, "Lucky to be alive, lucky to be alive," with a jovial spirit and a smile. At the time, I don't know that I appreciated this phrase he used. However, it has a whole new meaning to me today now that I know the gravity of the life they had experienced and escaped from.

Consequently, from both my parents' examples, I tend to operate with positivity as well. When hard times happen, I know that those times are not more difficult circumstances than my parents' lives were. When I have to push through something and work hard, I just do what's needed, because I saw my father willingly work hard because he loved his family and appreciated the opportunities of the United States. It is hard for me to understand those who get upset over the littlest things, the smallest inconveniences. I would much prefer to look on the bright side.

In my practice, you may recall that we have an ironclad rule: no gossip, drama, or negativity. We don't have time, in a busy practice, for drama queens, for backstabbing, or for anything but positive energy. Now, to be clear, tough times happen. People will disagree; people will have days when they are not at their best. But the amazing thing about cultivating a climate of positivity is that we support each other. We can lift up that team member when they have an off day, and we can all give each other that pep talk and encouragement when it's needed.

As someone who grew up in an immigrant family that experienced unimaginable hardships, I've learned the importance of maintaining a positive outlook, even in the face of adversity. My parents, despite everything they went through, always displayed gratitude and optimism, and that's something that has deeply influenced my approach to life and leadership. In my orthodontic practice, I strive to cultivate a positive and supportive culture where everyone feels valued and appreciated. Here are some of the ways I incorporate positivity into my practice:

- **Leading by example.** I believe that positivity starts at the top. I make a conscious effort to show up happy every day, even when I'm facing challenges. I can't expect my staff to come in with a positive attitude if I'm not leading by example. Leaders set the tone for the team. I remember, one time, having to let someone go because they were creating drama. They were in a supervisory position—and their example was not the one the team needed. Of course, we can try to lead someone toward the core values—but ultimately, the core values cannot be compromised on for long. Leadership must set the standard.
- **Focusing on strengths.** I try to focus on what people are good at instead of constantly telling them what they're doing wrong. As I discussed in the last chapter, it's essential to build a strengths-based team and to empower people to use their talents. Ultimately, a strengths-based approach is one of positivity. Maybe you have heard of the parenting concept of catching your child doing something good and praising that behavior as opposed to only reprimanding them when they are doing something wrong. It is the same idea—praise

what your team is doing right! Celebrate those wins. However, remember my point about courageous conversations. Caring for our people and teams sometimes means course corrections—and pushing toward the strengths you know your team can develop.

- **Practicing gratitude.** I encourage my team to appreciate what we have and to focus on the positive aspects of our work. They know the story of my family—and why practicing gratitude is so important to me. But practicing gratitude is also remembering to thank our coworkers for doing a great job—appreciating each other. "Please" and "Thank you" will never go out of fashion. I try to think of thoughtful ways to show my appreciation.
- **Promoting open communication.** I strive to overcommunicate. I encourage my team members to share their thoughts and ideas and to address any concerns they may have. Letting issues fester is a surefire way to ruin positivity in the workplace. As I previously shared, before I understood the basement of my strength of Harmony, I had a tendency to hope difficult things would just work out. I think at those times, I was both avoiding conflict and being an optimist. I have learned that optimism and positivity are great—but positivity without communication is just masking the issues at hand. Avoiding the difficult conversations never works, and people are not mind readers. Too often, miscommunications happen because we make assumptions, thinking the other person certainly understood what we meant. In addition, when there is a lack of communication, sometimes what fills the cracks is negativity. Which brings me to my next topic …

- **Addressing negativity.** The opposite of positivity is toxic negativity. I cannot overstate my zero-tolerance policy for gossip, drama, and negativity—it's so important to me, you will hear me say it again before the end of this book. Address negativity head-on, and communicate directly with each other to focus on finding solutions. My team has been with me long enough now that they know that if they have an issue with someone, the response will always be, "Have you discussed this with them?"

  Here's just one simple example: My team went on a trip last year. Many of them had been with the practice for many years, and they had a concern about a teammate. They actually came to me and said, "We do not want to gossip, and we do not think we are, but we are trying to problem-solve how to approach our colleague and let them know how we feel." Communication is *hard*, even for a team like mine that has practice and support. And it's especially hard as women—many of us were raised to be "nice," to not rock the boat. These conversations do not come comfortably, but this is why we must be courageous. When my team came to me on this trip, I was impressed that they had really thought about the difference between gossiping and problem-solving—they are two very different things, and I was proud to feel we had reached a milestone with their own reflection on the matter at hand.

- **Celebrating successes.** I make it a point to celebrate our practice's accomplishments, both big and small. Recognizing and appreciating the contributions of my team members helps to boost morale and create a sense of camaraderie. I also like to reward myself; I have come to recognize that caring for myself

> is important too. Positivity, to me, has meant taking a breath and realizing that it is OK to take a vacation without guilt, to celebrate successes with things that bring me happiness. We are all more positive when we have taken time for self-care. I will be honest: Maintaining positivity as a leader isn't always easy. There are times when I feel overwhelmed or stressed. That's when I rely on my support system, including my husband, my friends from dental school and residency, and my consulting group, to help me stay grounded and focused on the positive.

I have found myself in uncomfortable situations where my harmony and positivity are tested. In these cases, I try to remind myself that I am not the focus—the core values are. Even facing negative events should not disturb my own sense of positivity.

Ultimately, positivity is a choice. I can choose to focus on the challenges and obstacles in my path, or I can choose to focus on the opportunities and possibilities. By choosing to cultivate a positive mindset, I can create a workplace where everyone thrives and where we can provide the best possible care for our patients. Positivity has helped me create the culture I want, and it starts with me.

Integrity

My parents were always as good as their word—and they instilled in me that my word mattered too. That is integrity.

To me, integrity is how we behave when we think no one is watching. It was like my mother said about me going off to school in Boston. I may have been far from home, but God (and my own conscience) would know what I was doing.

When I saw integrity make our core values list at the practice, I was delighted. It conjured for me the image of my dad cleaning the donut shop on Christmas morning. Would anyone know if the donut shop wasn't spotless?

In fact, someone would know: my dad. That shop was a deep source of pride for him and for our family. So, he worked when it was difficult and tiring, when it would have been so much easier to simply take the day off. My mother was the same. No, we would *not* be opening our Christmas presents before Dad got back. The two of them took incredible pride in the store—in both its product and how people were treated, as well as in their hard work.

For me, this same commitment to excellence is reflected in the integrity of our practice. We do not cut corners, and if there is a problem (and there will always be problems), we address it right away. We value honesty, owning up to our mistakes and learning from them, and keeping our word.

As someone whose family overcame immense adversity, I've learned that integrity is essential for building trust, maintaining strong relationships, and achieving long-term success. It is a guiding principle that informs my decisions, shapes my leadership style, and defines my commitment to my patients, my team, and my community. Here's how integrity shows up in my life and my practice and leadership:

- **Honesty with patients.** I believe in being up-front and transparent with my patients about their treatment options, the potential risks and benefits, and the associated costs. I never try to upsell them on unnecessary procedures or make promises that I can't keep. I prioritize their well-being above all else. I treat people how I would want to be treated—and honesty is extremely important to me.

- **Ethical business practices.** I am committed to running my practice in an ethical and responsible manner. I never engage in deceptive or misleading practices. I am a doctor, first and foremost. That means wanting the best possible treatments for my individual patients. No two patients are identical! I make recommendations that I feel are in the best interest of each patient who walks in the door.
- **Fairness with employees.** I believe in treating my team members with respect and fairness. I provide them with a safe and supportive work environment, offer competitive wages and benefits, and recognize their contributions. I also empower them to make decisions and to take ownership of their work. I want them each to grow in their own strengths. Part of that is understanding that I need to trust them. I can't clone myself or be in four places at once. I want my team to be empowered to make the right choices independently.
- **Accountability.** I hold myself accountable for my actions and decisions. When I make a mistake, I own up to it, apologize, and take steps to correct it. I believe that accountability is essential for building trust and maintaining credibility. It also means my team needs to be accountable. Sometimes, people will make mistakes—and creating an environment where integrity is a core value means that owning up to mistakes will not be risky.

Integrity is essential for building a strong and sustainable business. My parents taught me this in how they ran their business and how they treated people. Integrity isn't something you try on like a sweater, and it's not just a set of rules or guidelines—it's a way of life. It's about striving to do what's right in every situation, even when it's difficult or unpopular. By prioritizing integrity in my personal and professional life, I can build strong relationships, create a positive impact on my community, and achieve lasting success.

Team Player

Over the many years before my team and I wrote "Team Player" on our whiteboard, I watched my father offer his help—whether it was teaching others about the donut shop business, hiring family members needing a job, or just lending a helping hand at church, he was someone who cared. Though he and my mom often ran the donut shop with minimal help, I think about how they went from strangers in an arranged marriage to this united team. Part of being a team is being supportive of one another, of lifting each other up when someone is down. My parents' strong marriage embodied this. And now, in my own marriage, I see my husband and me (and our village!) as a team—not to mention the very real team of my practice.

As someone deeply influenced by my parents' values of hard work, gratitude, and service to others, I've always understood the importance of teamwork, and I've worked diligently to cultivate a positive and supportive culture in my orthodontic practice. My approach to teamwork emphasizes open communication, mutual respect, and a shared commitment to our core values. Those core values are the glue of our team.

Why? Because every situation, even a difficult one, points us back to our core values. That's how to have the difficult conversations. If someone has a bad experience in our office, we go back to our core values. How did that experience occur? If an employee is having a bad day—or ten bad days (we all have our occasional off day, but to see that consistently is never what we hope for!)—I consider how the situation fits with our core values. Whenever we bring anyone new on to the team, I go through our core values and ask if they feel they can get on board with them. We all row together to lift our boat on the tide.

Stress is part of every job—there is no such thing as a stress-free job. But teamwork can lessen that stress. It is so heartwarming to hear everyone as they come in the door each morning, warmly greeting each other. We have a truly special place to work.

One of the key lessons I've learned is that micromanagement is a hallmark of a lack of teamwork. Teamwork, once again, demands that you trust your team members. Our strengths-based approach helps to create a more positive and supportive environment where everyone feels empowered to contribute their best.

As with positivity, I've also realized that clear communication is essential for effective teamwork. I make it a point in our practice to communicate my expectations and ensure that everyone understands their roles and responsibilities while encouraging open dialogue so that everyone feels comfortable sharing their thoughts and ideas.

Leading with empathy is another crucial aspect of my approach to teamwork. I try to be aware of the challenges that my team members face, both personally and professionally, and to offer support and understanding. For instance, when I took over the practice, I was aware that some mothers on my staff had difficulty getting to work early in the morning with their own kids' school schedules. So, I worked to create a more flexible schedule that accommodated their needs.

Building a strong team hasn't always been easy. Early in my career, I faced a challenging situation where a key team member was causing a lot of dissension—gossip, drama, backbiting, and negativity. Despite her skills and experience (which are, of course, valuable), I had to make the difficult decision to let her go in order to protect the team's culture. Although it was a painful experience, it ultimately strengthened the team and reinforced our commitment to a positive work environment. The team members who remained became even more protective of our culture, ensuring that gossip, drama, and negativity were quickly addressed.

Ultimately, for me, teamwork is about creating a community where everyone feels valued, supported, and empowered to achieve their full potential.

Pride in Your Work

Even if it meant my sister and I sleeping on flour sacks in the evenings, our family's donut shop was clean, and its products were delicious. When telling stories of the long hours my parents worked, I sometimes forget that they were creating something great. Even though they don't have a website, you can ask anyone or see the reviews on Yelp—their donuts are fresh, amazing, and served with a smile. I am proud of that, and of the shop! I don't know that I have told my parents this.

The pride my parents take in their work has echoed throughout my professional journey. They demonstrated a strong work ethic and a deep sense of responsibility, which shaped my approach to my orthodontic practice. I've cultivated a business environment where quality, commitment, and a sense of accomplishment are highly valued.

Sometimes, we see the pride in our work after the fact, not while we're in the thick of it. My parents get emotional with pride at the life they were able to create here. For me, I can think back on the story I told in chapter 1 about buying my practice—signing those loan papers with a trembling hand and inheriting a rundown satellite office, a practice with old x-rays and processes. When I compare that to my now-thriving practice of happy faces, shiny offices, and the latest technology, I am proud. I am proud that I am a trusted orthodontist in the communities where I practice. I am proud, as a first-generation American, of what I have accomplished (and I am not done yet!).

I'm proud of the work that I do, and I strive to instill that same sense of pride in my team. I believe that when people take pride in their work, they are more engaged, more productive, and more likely to deliver exceptional results.

I feel a responsibility to do my best for pretty much anyone that I come in contact with. It's not just work and family. Every single person has a unique story to tell. All of them have challenges that they've overcome, so how can we use those experiences and challenges to make our little micro world better?

When I reflect on what makes me most proud in my professional life, several key areas stand out. These aren't just abstract concepts—they're the tangible ways I measure whether I'm honoring the work ethic my parents modeled for me throughout my childhood. Each time I see my father's meticulous attention to his shop or recall my mother's dedication to ensuring every customer felt valued, I'm reminded of these essential aspects of pride in my work:

- **Quality of care**. I am committed to providing the highest-quality orthodontic care to my patients. I stay up to date with the latest advancements in the field and invest in technology that allows me to deliver the most effective and efficient treatment. I take pride in knowing that I am helping my patients achieve healthy, beautiful smiles that will last a lifetime. I take pride when I introduce new technologies that will improve the practice. And I take pride in the work I have put in with my practice consultant to better my leadership skills and the practice as a whole. These all impact our quality of care and make our practice successful.

- **Patient experience**. I want patients to feel valued, supported, and cared for throughout their orthodontic journey. I strive to create a warm and welcoming environment where patients feel comfortable and confident in the care they are receiving. I take a great deal of pride in hearing friendly voices calling out greetings to people as they walk in the door. I take pride in knowing people will leave such positive reviews of their experiences with us. It means we are living our core values.
- **Team culture**. I foster a positive and supportive team culture where everyone feels valued and respected. I empower my team members to take ownership of their work and to take pride in their contributions. I also encourage professional growth and development, providing opportunities for my team to expand their skills and knowledge. I could not be prouder of us all.

Ultimately, pride in our work is reflected in our teamwork too—it is how all our core values work together. A team that is proud of their workplace will have integrity and will pitch in as needed to help teammates. They will reflect positivity. In turn, with all these values working together, our service will be above and beyond.

These core values—service, positivity, integrity, teamwork, and pride—create a foundation for everything we do. They're not just words on a wall or concepts we discuss in team meetings; they're principles that guide our daily actions and decisions. When we live by these values, we create an environment where both our team and our patients can thrive.

But even the strongest core values require something essential to bring them to life: genuine connection with others. This is where the next chapter of my leadership journey began to unfold—discovering the transformative power of empathy. While our core values provide the structure, it's empathy that breathes life into them, allowing us to truly see and understand the people we serve and work alongside every day.

CHAPTER 7

Leading with Empathy

When we focus on others, our world expands.

~ DANIEL GOLEMAN

As I reflect on my journey as an orthodontist, a business owner, and a leader, I realize that one quality has been more crucial to my success than any other: *empathy.* I have always placed importance on understanding others' experiences, feelings, and perspectives. Because of the experiences of my parents and extended family, I try to walk through the world with gratitude and empathy (and to model this for my daughters). This is a gift in a world where people lose their serenity over losing a parking spot or waiting ten minutes for a table at a restaurant. Empathy for the people and the world around me, for those less fortunate than me, means I cannot have that impatience or intolerance. I wouldn't be my parents' daughter if I behaved that way.

Empathy is "understanding a person from their frame of reference rather than one's own, or vicariously experiencing that person's feelings, perceptions, and thoughts."[4] If you were ever told to walk a mile in someone else's shoes, that is empathy. As a Christian, the Bible is full of quotes that encapsulate empathy, such as John 15:12, one of the most famous biblical quotes: "This is my commandment, that you love one another as I have loved you."

Importantly, leading with empathy is not just a management technique; it's a way of being. It's about recognizing the humanity in everyone I encounter, whether they're a patient, a team member, or a stranger on the street. It's about putting myself in their shoes, trying to understand their challenges and aspirations, and responding with compassion and understanding. For me, empathy creates a safe space where people feel seen, heard, and valued.

Empathy Rooted in My Family History

Growing up, I witnessed firsthand the challenges my parents faced as immigrants in a new country. They struggled to learn English, navigate unfamiliar customs, and overcome prejudice and discrimination. They worked tirelessly to provide for our family, often holding multiple jobs and sacrificing their own needs to ensure that my siblings and I had every opportunity to succeed. But I think I am probably like most people. I could not fully understand their experiences. I was, after all, born into freedom. However, I was an observant enough child to see how my parents navigated their difficulties and treated people.

I also know that those challenges also meant some very hard decisions. I don't think there are many parents who enjoy saying no to their kids. Recently, my family and I were in Fort Wayne for my daughter's volleyball tournament. We were on the north side of town,

4 American Psychological Association, s.v. "empathy," *APA Dictionary of Psychology*, accessed February 20, 2025, https://dictionary.apa.org/empathy.

where all the "really nice homes" were when I was growing up. We drove by one specific neighborhood, and I told my girls I remembered looking at a house in this nice neighborhood with my parents at one point when they'd been thinking about moving. But my mother told me that after they did the calculations for how much it would cost to send me and my sister to college, they would not have had enough money. So they decided not to buy the house. All their decisions were made with empathy and care for their children and relatives.

Their experiences instilled in me a profound sense of empathy for anyone who has faced adversity. I especially feel for women and children living with or escaping abuse, and I know my mother's heart breaks seeing refugees the world over. Regardless of where they are coming from, refugees are experiencing a sense of displacement and fear I would not wish on anyone.

I learned to appreciate the importance of kindness, understanding, and support, and I resolved to create a world where everyone feels valued and respected. My parents chose to never be bitter. Instead, they chose to be givers. They maintained their dignity in the face of shut doors or unwelcoming people—and they were the recipients of deep empathy and kindness from their sponsor church. My parents then took the opportunity to pay it forward by helping others.

Empathy in My Orthodontic Practice

As an orthodontist, I recognize that my patients are not just teeth and mouths; they are people with unique stories, fears, and aspirations; they are part of a family. Many of them, especially children, are anxious about coming to the orthodontist. My staff and I always try to make them comfortable and at ease. I make it a point to connect with each patient on a personal level, taking the time to listen to their concerns, understand their goals, and address their anxieties. I strive to create a safe and welcoming environment where my patients feel comfortable expressing themselves and asking questions.

I remember when I was a resident, one young patient was particularly nervous about getting braces. She had heard horror stories from her friends about the pain and discomfort involved, and she was convinced that the experience would be unbearable. I sat down with her and patiently explained the procedure, answering all of her questions and addressing her fears. I showed her the braces and demonstrated how they worked, and I reassured her that we would do everything possible to make her comfortable.

During the procedure, I checked in with her frequently, asking her how she was feeling and adjusting the treatment as needed to minimize any discomfort. I praised her for her bravery and cooperation, and I made sure she knew that she was in control. By the end of the appointment, she was smiling and relieved. My staff uses the same reassuring approach today.

This experience reinforced my belief that empathy is essential for providing high-quality orthodontic care. By taking the time to understand my patients' fears and anxieties, I can build trust, create a positive experience, and ultimately achieve better outcomes.

Empathy for My Team

Empathy is equally important in my relationships with my team members. I recognize that they are individuals with their own lives, challenges, and aspirations, and I strive to create a supportive and empowering work environment where they can thrive. I try to be an empathetic boss. My employees are mostly women, and many are moms.

I make a point of getting to know each of my team members on a personal level, learning about their families, their hobbies, and their goals. I listen to their concerns, provide them with regular feedback, and offer them opportunities for professional growth and development. Recently, my consultant worked with each of my individual staff members in a goal-setting meeting based on each person's strengths. This is just one of the ways I make sure everyone at our practice knows that I value their unique contributions and that I am committed to their success.

I also understand that my team members sometimes face challenges outside of work that can impact their performance. Whether it's a sick child, a family emergency, or a personal struggle, I try to be understanding and supportive, offering them flexibility and assistance as needed.

When I realized that many of the mothers who worked for me were finding it difficult to get to work on time with the set hours of the office, I considered the situation with empathy, and I knew that it wasn't about not wanting to get to work; they had constraints with their children. I knew the village needed to be led by a woman entrepreneur. So, I implemented flexible scheduling options to accommodate those needs. It's important for me to acknowledge people's lives and families; work is not the only important thing.

I also try to check in with my team members regularly and ask how they're doing. I try to notice how people are feeling and respond with the appropriate support. For instance, I've learned to ask the question, "What do you need from me?" As a leader, it is one of the most important questions to ask. Sometimes, that means just listening; other times, it means finding ways to help team members, such as offering extra training.

One of the most effective ways I have found to lead with empathy is, again, to focus on each team member's unique strengths and talents. The very mindset of a strengths-based approach is empathetic. When we recognize what makes other people special, we see people in the most positive light—a trait my parents always had. Focusing on strengths is a way to cultivate a more productive and enjoyable work experience.

For example, I have a team member who is a natural communicator. She has a gift for connecting with people, building rapport, and explaining complex information in a clear and concise manner. To recognize her strengths, I assigned her the role of patient educator, in which she can use her communication skills to help patients understand their treatment options and make informed decisions about their oral health. I also have team members who are highly organized and detail-oriented. I have someone who excels at managing schedules, coordinating appointments, and ensuring that everything runs smoothly behind the scenes. It's a bit like chess, determining which person fits where and what their special skills and strengths are.

By recognizing and leveraging each team member's unique strengths, I can create a more well-rounded and effective team, where everyone feels valued, empowered, and engaged. But it is the skill of empathy that allows me to see the talents of each person.

The Four-Way Win: Leading with Empathy

One of the ways in which I incorporate empathy into my leadership is with the concept of the four-way win developed by Stewart Friedman (a founding director at Wharton's Leadership program), who wrote a book years ago called *Total Leadership: Be a Better Leader, Have a Richer Life*.

Friedman's four-way win is about balancing work, home, community, and self. It recognizes that all four domains are important to each of us in order to have a balanced life. This requires constant adjustment and a willingness to prioritize self-care (not easy for us type A's!). For me, looking at the four-way win, I could immediately see how I prioritized work. After all, I had grown up in a household where hard work was simply what we did. I never really gave working hard much of a thought—it was just ingrained in me.

Home was also obvious to me. After all, I came back to Indiana from Boston when I was ready to establish my own practice. I am a devoted wife, mom, and daughter. I could not imagine not returning to my roots and raising my family around my parents.

Community, to me, was my orthodontic practice—my team and my patients—my church community, and the various places where I hope I make an impact.

But that *last* win has taken me some time. Self. When you are raised as a first-generation American, often, that immigrant drive is so ingrained in you that learning to be empathetic to yourself is a lesson that is needed. I have had to learn that the four-way win includes me!

I've also learned that it's OK to ask for help. (For some first-generation folks, *help* is a four-letter word!) These days, I rely on my parents, in-laws, friends, church, nanny, work team, and consulting group for support.

Addressing Conflict with Empathy

Even in the most harmonious work environments, conflict is inevitable. Disagreements can arise between team members, misunderstandings can occur, and tensions can escalate. As a leader, it is my responsibility to address these conflicts in a fair, empathetic, and constructive manner.

When conflict arises, my first step is to listen to all sides of the story. I try to understand each person's perspective, acknowledging their feelings and validating their experiences. I avoid taking sides or assigning blame, instead focusing on finding a solution that is fair and equitable to everyone involved.

But one mistake as an empathetic person would be to get in the middle. When you're empathetic, you want to help, but the best way to help others who are struggling with one another is not to try to resolve the issue for them but to encourage open communication and direct dialogue between the parties involved. I expect my team members to address their concerns directly with each other rather than complain behind their backs. I remember one of my staff members actually thanking me for pushing her to have the courageous conversations. Learning how to have and push through the conversations helped her not only at work but in her personal and family life too. How many of us avoid these courageous conversations? If the conflict cannot be resolved through direct communication, I or my management team will mediate the situation, facilitating a discussion and helping the parties involved to find common ground. I use my communication skills to clarify expectations, set boundaries, and encourage compromise. I remind everyone of our core values (again, when we share values, we row together) and how we can best serve our patients and each other.

I believe that conflict, when handled properly, can be an opportunity for growth and learning. By addressing conflicts with empathy, fairness, and open communication, I can strengthen my team, improve our relationships, and create a more positive and productive work environment.

The Power of Showing Up

Ultimately, leading with empathy is about showing up for my patients, my team members, and my community. It's about being present, engaged, and fully invested in whatever I am doing. It's about giving my best effort, even when I don't feel like it, and it's about taking responsibility for my actions.

Showing up also means being willing to be vulnerable, to share my own struggles and imperfections, and to connect with others on a human level. It means being authentic, genuine, and true to myself. I have learned that when I show up with empathy, compassion, and authenticity, I can create a ripple effect that transforms my practice, my team, and my community. I can inspire others to be more kind, more understanding, and more supportive, and I can create a world where everyone feels valued, respected, and empowered to achieve their full potential. It's one reason I started a book club with my team. When we share authentically, it not only teaches us leadership and teamwork; it also makes us more empathetic toward each other.

The Enduring Grace of Empathy

As I conclude this chapter, I am filled with a profound sense of gratitude for the enduring grace of empathy. It has been a guiding force in my life, shaping my relationships, informing my decisions, and defining my leadership style.

Empathy is not just a soft skill; it's a superpower. It allows me to connect with others on a deeper level, to understand their needs and aspirations, and to inspire them to achieve their full potential. It has helped me build a thriving orthodontic practice, a supportive and engaged team, and a community where everyone feels valued and respected.

I hope that this chapter has inspired you to embrace the power of empathy in your own life. May you find the courage to put yourself in others' shoes, to listen with an open heart, and to respond with compassion and understanding. For in the end, it is empathy that connects us, that heals us, and that empowers us to create a better world for all.

CHAPTER 8
Full Circle

Parents aren't the people you come from. They're the people you want to be, when you grow up.

~ JODI PICOULT

As the new year of 2025 approached, I found myself preparing for a remarkable journey that was more than just a vacation; it was a pilgrimage to honor my parents and their incredible story of survival and resilience. I was taking my parents back to Thailand and Cambodia, a trip that felt like a culmination of their sacrifices and a way for me to show my daughters their heritage as well as to connect with that world myself. It was our chance to see and experience Thailand and Cambodia through my parents' eyes.

It felt like we were coming full circle. My parents' story started thousands of miles away, and that's where we would travel—only this time, I would be taking my husband and my own children.

Planning the Trip

Planning a trip for seven people, including my sister and parents, required meticulous attention to detail. It's my nature to be detail-oriented, but this was a huge undertaking. There were plane tickets to book, itineraries to arrange, and the added complexity of ensuring my parents' comfort and accessibility throughout the journey. To avoid strenuous walks through airports (and trust me, there are not too many ways to travel direct to the places we planned to visit), I arranged for wheelchair transfers and their luggage to be checked, wanting to make everything as smooth as possible for them. It was a little overwhelming at times, juggling the logistics of international travel with the emotional weight of revisiting my parents' homeland.

Sometimes, when you are planning something huge and important to you, you are so focused on the planning that you are not even processing the emotions of it all. I'm not sure I fully realized the enormity of our trip until we were flying over the lush jungles of that part of Asia.

Topographical map of Cambodia. Source: WorldAtlas.com

As a solo orthodontist, it was also very tricky for me to leave my practice for an extended length of time. I had to prepare my team for my absence—and after writing this book and thinking about core values and *StrengthsFinder 2.0*, it was very gratifying to me to know this was possible. I could trust and rely on my team. I arranged for an assistant to handle emergencies and made sure all patient cases were up to date before I left. I planned to check in daily using the DentalMonitoring AI platform to oversee my patients' progress. My office manager would try to run interference and prevent me from being messaged too much. Here, once again, my commitment to best practices, efficiencies, and technology meant that I could actually consider being across the world as a business owner. Having a team where I knew their strengths and knew I could trust them to handle the practice while I was gone was really a testament to the years of work and consulting that transformed my practice.

As we planned the trip, I also wanted my daughters, Grace and Vivienne, to be involved and excited about our big adventure. I asked Grace and Vivienne to be my "little helpers" with Ama and Kong (Grandma and Grandpa), hoping they would embrace the role with enthusiasm, which they did. Because I grew up around older generations—my parents, grandparents, and great uncles and aunts—I truly believe that children growing up around their elders is a gift. This deepened my excitement about this trip. I wanted us all to remember and treasure the memories forever. I know that, as children, my daughters could not fully grasp all we did on our journey, but they experienced this trip with their grandparents, and it is something I know they will one day truly treasure—I certainly do.

Returning to Thailand

As we touched down in Thailand, I could sense a mix of emotions in my parents. Excitement, nostalgia, and perhaps a hint of trepidation filled the air. It was a homecoming, but also a reminder of the hardships they had endured before finding refuge in the United States.

As an adult, I thought I understood my parents' story. The idea for the trip had been brewing for a while. My parents hadn't been back to Cambodia in over twenty years, and I felt it was important for them to reconnect with their roots while they were still healthy enough to travel such a long distance. I also felt it was important for me to understand their history. That I was still writing this book at the time made it more special.

Even before we arrived in Cambodia and Thailand, the trip was eye-opening. At the airports, the wheelchair assistance helped guide us through, but it was also a reminder of the challenges my parents face as they get older. In Cambodia, the airport experience highlighted a completely different kind of challenge: the treatment of my Cambodian cousins. When we left, my cousins were not allowed to enter the airport to say goodbye, being treated as second-class citizens. This was a stark reminder of the inequalities that persist in the world and the privilege I often take for granted. Experiencing that with them afforded me the smallest glimpse of the hardships they faced, of the active control over people that still persists in the world.

Our first stop was Bangkok, Thailand, where we spent the first five days of our trip before traveling to Cambodia, Phuket, and then back to Thailand for our final day. Flying in, the modern skyscrapers and towers were no doubt different from my parents' memories, as they had been mostly confined to a refugee camp in Thailand. Most of the buildings are pale—they look almost white from the sky.

My mother had a list of things she wanted to do and places she wanted to see. I hired a guide to take us around. We visited markets and Chinatown, whose entrance is marked by a colorful *paifang* (those large gates, often red and brightly painted, that typically mark the entrance to Chinatowns all over the world). Bangkok's Chinatown is quite large, with twisting alleyways and secret markets for everything from Chinese herbs to electronics. It was almost overwhelming, with the scents of delicious food and bright colors.

Driving around, we caught glimpses of the famed Thai Elephant Building, as well as the tallest building in Thailand, King Power Mahanakhon, which reflects light and looks pixelated, like a real-life video game. Modern Thailand is iconic. I had even booked a relaxing spa visit at Le Méridien resort for our last night of the trip, but we arrived from Phuket too late to experience it, much to my patient husband's chagrin. But before Phuket, we had an important journey to make first. It was time to fly to Cambodia.

Cambodia: Landmines and Khmer Rouge

We visited Cambodia for three days. On one of the days, I took a side trip with my cousin, my husband, and our two girls to the Cambodia Landmine Museum in Siem Reap, near Angkor Wat. The museum was founded by Aki Ra (we got to meet him), a former child soldier who was forced to plant landmines for the Khmer Rouge regime. After the regime fell, he began demining the countryside himself as a young man and eventually started an organization dedicated to the cause. In addition, he adopted children orphaned by mines.

Visiting the Landmine Museum was a powerful and disturbing experience. The museum displayed countless deactivated landmines and told the stories of the victims. I learned that there are *still* an estimated six million landmines in Cambodia, rendering vast swaths of land unusable for farming and posing a constant threat to the population. It is not unusual to see people missing limbs in Cambodia—even young children. The war may be over, but the dangerous landmines persist.

As we looked at deactivated landmines, the stories of my parents, grandmother, and extended family became more vivid. I thought of the young soldier who had been blown up while leading my grandmother to Thailand, someone else's son she grieved so dearly. One false step and a life was ended. To think that six million of these death mines remain is horrifying.

In the center courtyard of the museum is a pagoda-like structure with a red-tile roof and open on all sides. Inside this pagoda are all of the different varieties of landmines that were used in Cambodia. There is also a residential school for orphaned children.

Aki Ra's life is a reflection of Cambodia's tragic past—the past of my parents. Conscripted into the Khmer Rouge army at a mere five years old, he later joined the Vietnamese and Cambodian armies before dedicating his life to removing landmines by hand in the 1990s. His collection of deactivated explosives (remember, six *million* still remain—*six million*) became the foundation for the museum, which now serves as both an educational center and a rehabilitation facility for landmine victims, particularly orphaned children. The facility provides housing, education, and vocational training, giving these individuals a chance at a better future.

Aki Ra's work has extended beyond the museum itself. He was named a CNN Hero of the Year for his work. Through his NGO, Cambodian Self Help Demining, Aki Ra and his team continue to clear landmines in rural areas, making villages safe for farming and daily life.

Aki Ra was at the museum when we visited. Meeting him and hearing his story firsthand was incredibly moving. He explained Cambodia's history, including its fight with Vietnam and how Pol Pot took over. The country was ravaged by fighting for thirty-five years. The Cambodian people felt stuck between a dictator starving them and the Vietnam army trying to invade. These were the conditions my parents had faced. I was so moved by his story.

It was eerie to be at the museum. The experience made me appreciate the simple things in life, such as being able to walk without fear and having access to safe land. Just like appreciating food and having gratitude for each meal, seeing the museum sealed the connection in my mind of just how it is my parents could be so humbled by life, so appreciative of the little things. I was very quiet there, just observing and trying to use my skills of empathy to imagine my parents' experiences.

I'll never forget what I learned at the museum about the Khmer Rouge's atrocities and Cambodia's history, including the fact that after the Khmer Rouge regime fell, some of its members still ended up in government positions. This sort of corruption, which I've also heard my mother talk about over the years, saddened me.

I also learned more about the bombings by the United States during the Vietnam War. The guide explained that the Nixon administration had carpet-bombed Cambodia. This information put my mom's stories of the war into perspective, as she described having to hide underground from the bombs. In fact, hiding from bombs was the reason both my parents had to abandon their education as children. Once again, I realized that my empathy for children and love for them—my very career as an orthodontist—were impacted by my understanding that children are innocent in any situation, especially in war, displacement, or other unfortunate circumstances.

I had booked a house for all of us to stay in with my cousins so we could really reconnect—their experiences were so different from my own, again emphasizing how much I appreciate what my parents went through to create a life for themselves and their family. I had booked the house thinking it would be a special experience, but it was more of a tropical, natural setting, surrounded by greenery and rice fields. My dad joked that my aunt would think we were crazy for staying in the middle of the jungle!

The countryside of Cambodia is very lush. The jungle areas are wild and overgrown. The jungles are also *full* of snakes of all kinds—constrictors and venomous ones alike. I can't say I was thrilled about that! But I also hadn't really considered that the oppressiveness of the wild setting, the thickness of the vegetation, would stir up negative emotions and memories for my parents, in addition to their fond memories of childhood before the atrocities began.

For me, seeing expanses of lush jungles and rice fields was exotic—but I, too, could feel how suffocating it might seem, especially at night. The jungle is a cacophony of animals and birds. And it's *dark.* Very dark. In our Western world, we are so used to light—from stores, streetlights, restaurants, neighboring houses, etc. The jungle is dark as midnight itself. I could not even imagine leaving in the middle of the suffocating blackness to try to make it to Thailand, trying to avoid the dangerous creatures that lurked within, not to mention the fear of landmines, soldiers, and detection.

Beyond the historical sites and the jungle, I witnessed the poverty that still plagues Cambodia. It was a stark reminder of the disparities between the developed and developing worlds. I felt a sense of sadness and frustration that my cousins were still living in such difficult circumstances.

I thought about my parents' constant reminders to be grateful for the life we have in the States. I realized that, growing up, I didn't fully grasp the extent of their sacrifices and the horrors they had endured. All those times my father had told me to be grateful that we lived in the United States, I hadn't really understood. *Sure, sure, Dad.* Now, seeing the conditions in Cambodia firsthand made me appreciate the opportunities and freedoms we have in the States.

Our guide in Bangkok told us more about the political situation in Cambodia. The current prime minister of Cambodia is the son of the previous prime minister, who'd held the position for twenty-four years. Opposition is impossible. The day before we had returned to Bangkok, the opposition party leader had been gunned down in the middle of the day on a bus from Siem Reap to Thailand. Again, my parents' appreciation for the United States made so much sense. My mother's feelings about Cambodia have changed over the years. She said she doesn't miss it, partly because of the corruption, and at this point, she has lived more of her life in the United States than in Cambodia.

We ended our trip in Phuket, Thailand. It is a jewel alongside blue-green water, and after facing the stark realities of Cambodia, it was a nice respite for us all.

Gratitude

This trip to Cambodia and Thailand was an unforgettable experience that profoundly impacted me. I witnessed in a new way the struggles and hardships that my parents had endured, and I gained a newfound appreciation for their resilience and determination. I was reminded of the importance of gratitude, not just for the big things in life, but for the everyday blessings that we often take for granted.

I started to better understand why my parents had always told me to be grateful. They wanted me to appreciate the opportunities and freedoms that were not available to them in Cambodia. I realized that I want my kids to understand what my parents went through. I don't want them to take their privileged life for granted.

The trip to Cambodia and Thailand brought my life full circle. It connected me to my family's past and gave me a deeper understanding of their sacrifices and struggles. It reinforced the importance of gratitude and the need to appreciate the blessings in my life. And it inspired me to share my family's story with others, in the hopes that it might inspire them to overcome their own challenges and to never take their freedoms for granted.

The most emotional part of the trip was leaving my cousins in Cambodia. It was difficult to say goodbye, knowing that they might never have the opportunity to leave. The strict immigration laws make it nearly impossible for them to come to the United States. I even emailed governors and senators to advocate for my cousins but was told that they were denied due to the Cambodian government's requirements. We tried to move forward with the sponsorship process, but when my cousins' dad died, there was no longer a direct line allowing them to be sponsored to the States, though we were already in the middle of the process when he passed. After that, my other uncle tried to get them work visas to get them here, but they were denied because they didn't have enough land or money in the bank. The government there dictates that you cannot leave unless you have significant money or land, because they think you might otherwise not come back (and if you don't, they will seize your belongings).

My husband also felt bad that my cousins couldn't enter the airport and wanted to find a way to bring them to the States. It is a heartbreak we carry with us, and we continue to hope for some future in which they can come here.

Throughout the trip, I observed my parents with a fresh perspective. I saw their reactions to familiar sights, sounds, and flavors, and I gained a deeper understanding of their past. One of the most moving aspects of the trip was witnessing the interaction between my parents and my daughters. I know they were creating priceless memories.

As our journey came to an end, I felt a sense of gratitude and fulfillment. I had honored my parents, connected with my heritage, and created lasting memories with my daughters. The trip had not only enriched my life but had also given me a renewed sense of purpose and direction for the future.

ptember 9, 1980 Vol. 3 No. 19
aing Relatives Arrive
Free at last!
Taing relatives begi

CONCLUSION

The Enduring Grace of Family

As I sit here, reflecting on the journey that has led to these final words, my heart is full. Writing this book has been more than just a project; it's been a pilgrimage through my own life, a deep dive into the roots that have sustained me, and an exploration of the lessons learned from the most influential people in my world: my parents. Their story, etched in courage, sacrifice, and unwavering faith, has shaped the very essence of who I am. My own resilience is rooted in their examples of courage, family, and the power of showing up every day.

As author Elif Shafak so beautifully wrote, "The past lives within the present, and our ancestors breathe through our children."[5] I see that truth in my own daughters, in their tenacity, their empathy, and their unyielding spirit. They carry within them the legacy of my parents, the echoes of a history marked by both unimaginable hardship and incredible triumph.

This book has been an attempt to capture the essence of that legacy, to distill the wisdom gleaned from a lifetime of watching my

---

5 Elif Shafak, *The Bastard of Istanbul* (Dar Al Adab, 2024).

parents navigate the complexities of life with grace and grit. It has been about understanding the roots that have anchored me, the values that have guided me, and the unwavering support of family that has propelled me forward.

Courage as the Bedrock

As I arrive at the end of this book, I remain convinced that if there is one trait that defines my parents, it is courage. It was courage that had propelled them to flee the horrors of the Khmer Rouge regime—to leave behind everything they knew and embark on a perilous journey toward an unknown future. It was courage that had sustained them through the refugee camps, through the loneliness and isolation of being strangers in a foreign land. And it was courage that had empowered them to build a new life from scratch, to overcome language barriers, cultural differences, and the sting of prejudice.

Their courage is not the kind that makes headlines or earns medals. It is the quiet, persistent courage of showing up every day, of facing adversity with unwavering resolve, and of choosing hope over despair. It is the courage to believe in the face of doubt, to persevere in the face of setbacks, and to never give up on the dream of a better future.

The Indelible Bond of Family

Family is the cornerstone of my life, the anchor that keeps me grounded amid the storms. My parents' love for each other and for their children has been the driving force behind their every decision—their unwavering commitment to providing us with a better life than they had.

In the countless hours they spent at the donut shop, sacrificing their own comfort and well-being to ensure that my sister and I had everything we needed, they missed holidays, birthdays, and school events, but their sacrifices were a tangible expression of their love. Like many a teenager, I didn't realize that the reason my father was not in the stands at my volleyball game was *love.* My parents sacrificed so much for their family—silently.

Their example taught me the importance of prioritizing family, of nurturing relationships, and of creating a home filled with love and support. I strive to emulate that in my own family, making time for my daughters, being present in their lives, and creating memories that will last a lifetime. I get to have those moments with my daughters because my parents worked 365 days a year to create a life for us.

The Power of Showing Up Every Day

My parents never took a day off. They showed up day after day (after day!) to the donut shop. They showed up when they were exhausted, when they were discouraged, and when they would rather have been anywhere else (though, to be honest, I am not sure if either of them would say that!). They instilled in me the understanding that success is not a matter of luck or talent alone, but of consistent effort, unwavering dedication, and the willingness to show up, even when it's hard. Maybe especially when it's hard.

That lesson has been invaluable in my own life, particularly in the early years of my orthodontic practice. There were days when I felt overwhelmed by the challenges, when I questioned my abilities, and when I secretly wondered if I should give up. But then I would think of my parents, of their unwavering commitment to their business, and I would find the strength to keep going.

Showing up also means being present, being engaged, and being fully invested in whatever you are doing. It means giving your best effort, even when you don't feel like it, and it means taking responsibility for your actions. It is a commitment to excellence, a dedication to service, and a willingness to go the extra mile.

My daughters are growing up with great privilege. But I am sure to make clear to them that excellence is what is expected. Sometimes, school will be hard—but then that is the time to work harder. They know they are deeply loved, but they also know that I want them to push themselves to the best of their abilities.

Gratitude as a Guiding Light

Despite the hardships they endured, my parents never harbored bitterness or resentment. Instead, they embraced gratitude as a way of life, focusing on the blessings they had been given rather than dwelling on the injustices they had suffered. I feel like that is one of the biggest themes I saw as I wrote this book.

They were grateful for the opportunity to escape the horrors of Cambodia, for the kindness of strangers who helped them along the way, and for the chance to build a new life in the United States. They were grateful for their children, for their health, and for the simple joys of everyday life.

Their gratitude was contagious, shaping my own perspective and instilling in me a deep appreciation for the blessings in my own life. I am grateful for my family, for my friends, for my career, and for the opportunities I have been given. I am also grateful for the challenges I have faced, for they have made me stronger, more resilient, and more compassionate.

Faith as an Unwavering Compass

Faith has been an integral part of my parents' journey, providing them with strength, hope, and guidance through the darkest of times. My mother's story of finding God despite the Khmer Rouge regime is a testament to the power of faith to transcend even the most unimaginable suffering.

My parents' faith was not just a set of religious beliefs; it was a way of life, shaping their values, their actions, and their relationships. It was a belief in something bigger than themselves, a trust in a higher power, and a commitment to living a life of purpose and meaning.

I have carried that faith with me throughout my life, finding comfort and strength in times of uncertainty and drawing inspiration from its teachings. Faith has guided my decisions, shaped my leadership style, and instilled in me a deep sense of responsibility to give back to my community. From my first mission trip to my commitment to my church today, faith has been a compass guiding me toward true north.

The Journey Back Home

The trip to Cambodia and Thailand was a transformative experience, a chance to reconnect with my heritage, to honor my parents, and to share their story with my daughters. It was a journey into the past, a celebration of the present, and a testament to the enduring power of family.

I watched my parents as they revisited places of years ago, as they shared memories of their childhood, and as they reconnected with relatives they had not seen in decades. I saw their emotions as they grappled with the complexities of their past, with the pain of loss and the joy of reunion.

I also saw the impact of my parents' story on my daughters, as they began to understand the sacrifices their grandparents had made and to appreciate the opportunities they had been given. I watched as my girls formed bonds with their Cambodian cousins, as they learned about what is, to them, a different culture, and as they began to develop a sense of global awareness.

That journey back to Cambodia and Thailand reinforced the importance of gratitude, resilience, and the need to appreciate the blessings in life. I want my girls to understand what my parents went through so they don't take their privileged life for granted. I know that, for me, it has helped to keep me grounded.

Core Values as Guiding Principles

As a leader, I believe in the importance of defining and living by a set of core values. These values serve as a compass, guiding our decisions, shaping our actions, and defining our culture.

In my orthodontic practice, we have identified five core values that reflect our commitment to excellence, service, and integrity. I am so grateful that my team and I came up with these values together—and that we live these values in the day-to-day of our service to the community—and each other.

These values are not just words on a wall; they are the foundation of our practice, shaping our interactions with patients, guiding our decisions, and defining our culture. We strive to live by these values every day, creating a workplace where everyone feels valued, respected, and empowered to achieve their full potential.

The Power of Strengths-Based Leadership

Discovering strengths-based leadership has revolutionized my approach to managing my team. I am thrilled to share its importance on these pages. By focusing on each individual's unique talents and abilities, I have been able to create a more positive, productive, and fulfilling work environment.

The StrengthsFinder assessment revealed that my top strengths are Harmony, Consistency, Futuristic, Empathy, and Developer. At first, I didn't see how some of these could fit into a leadership style at all. I always thought that a leader should be direct, decisive, and maybe even a bit demanding, not someone who valued harmony and connection. I soon realized, though, that these weren't weaknesses; they were my greatest assets if I learned to use them in the right ways.

I have found that this approach to leadership not only makes my team happier and more engaged; it also makes them more productive and creative. When we're not busy worrying about office gossip or drama, we can focus on what matters most: our patients.

A Sixth-Grade Graduation Speech

Finally, I was recently asked to speak at a sixth-grade graduation. I had to think about what it was I wanted to share—what message did I want to deliver to these students? While contemplating my speech, I realized I had something relatable to share. I wanted to tell the kids that it's possible to be successful even if your parents don't speak English or didn't go to college. Success has no limits. I wanted to encourage them to believe in themselves and to take advantage of the opportunities available to them in the United States. A friend who is a teacher once told me that too many kids think they can't achieve something because they don't have certain advantages.

As I prepared my speech, I realized that, growing up, I had felt like I had something to prove because my parents weren't like everyone else's. But my parents always told me that I lived in the best country and could do anything I wanted. In fact, as I conclude this book, I am filled with a profound sense of gratitude for the enduring grace of family. My parents' love, their sacrifices, and their unwavering belief in me have shaped the very essence of who I am. Their story is a testament to the power of courage, resilience, and faith, and it is a legacy that I am proud to carry forward.

I hope that this book has inspired you to reflect on your own roots, to appreciate the lessons learned from your ancestors, and to embrace the power of family in your own life. May you find strength in the face of adversity, hope in the midst of despair, and the unwavering support of loved ones to guide you on your journey.

For in the end, it is family that sustains us, that anchors us, and that empowers us to become the best versions of ourselves. And it is the enduring grace of family that makes all things possible.

GALLERY

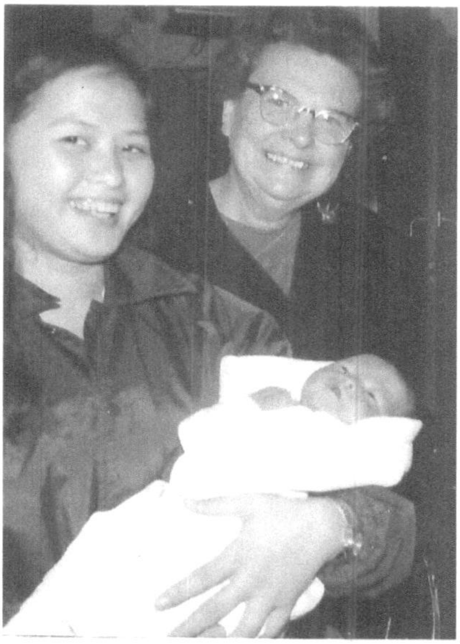

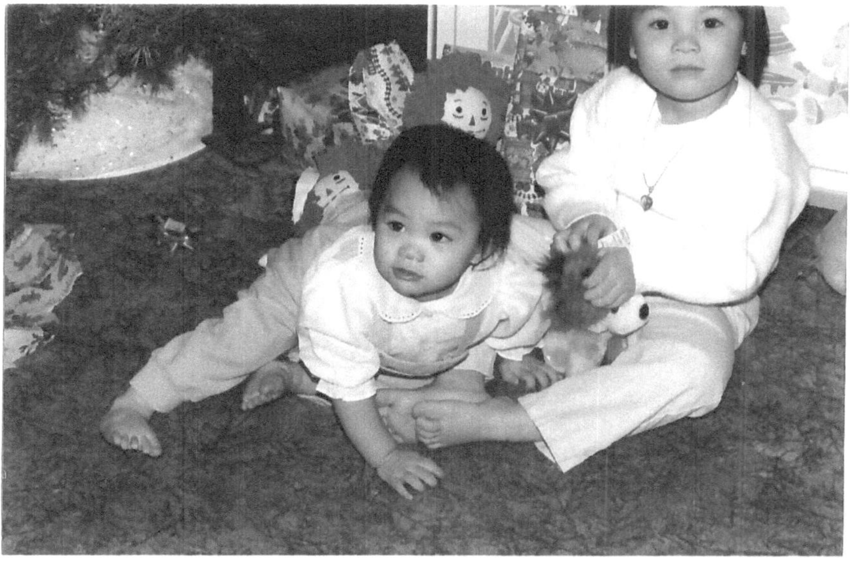

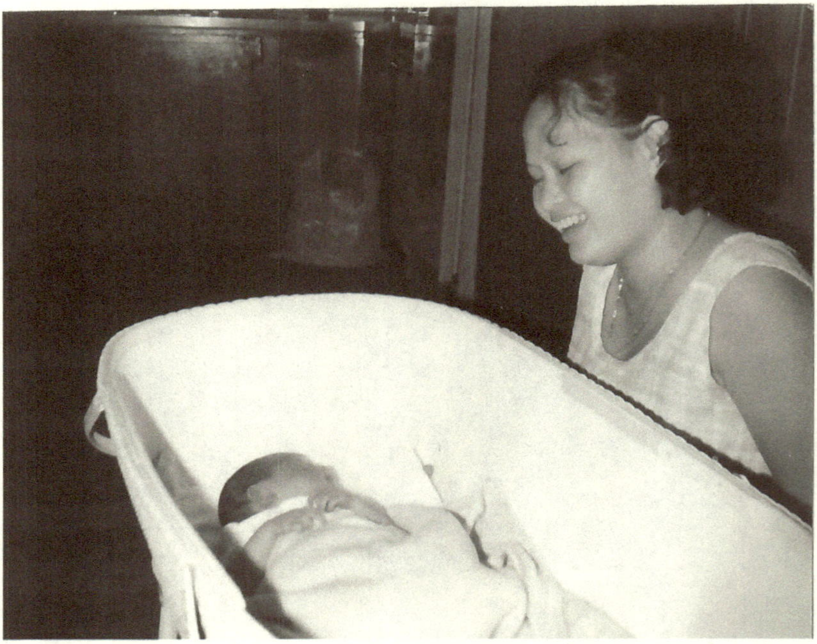

Glenbrook Square

olan mills
© 88

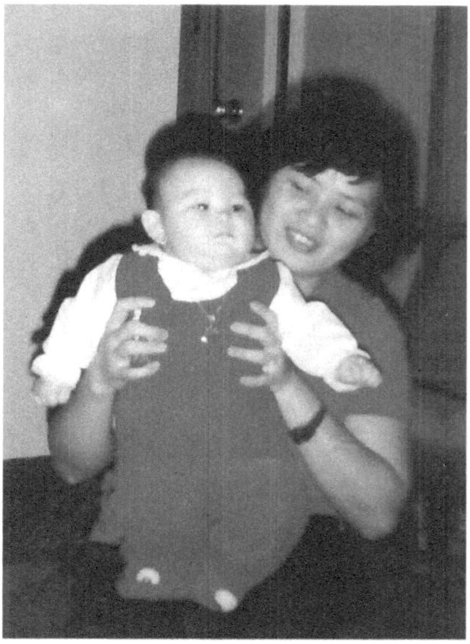

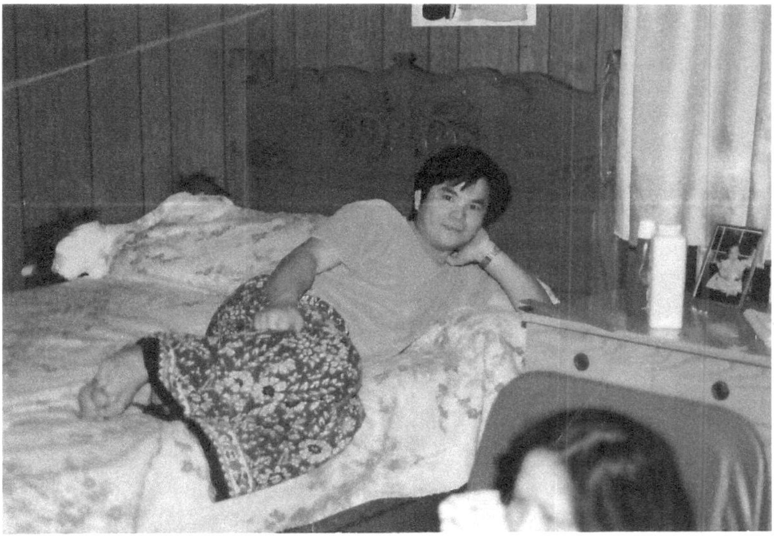

olan mills

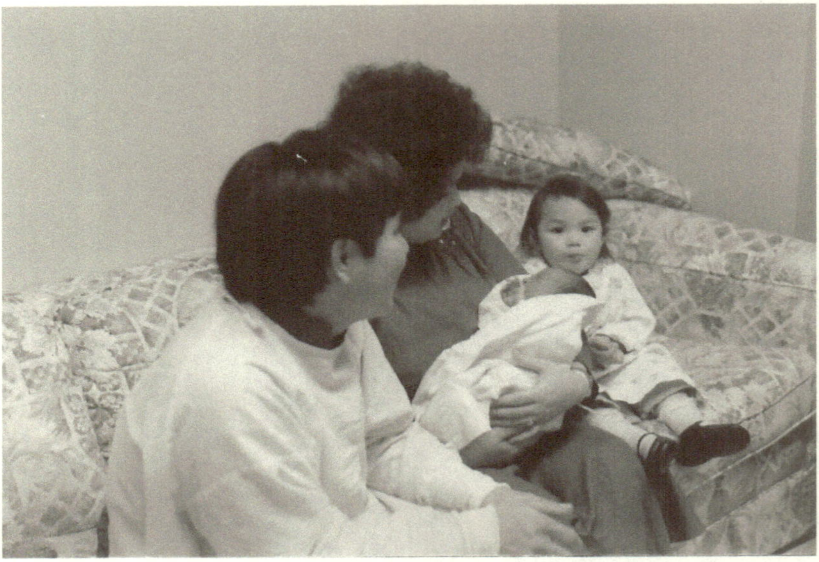

JUNE
86

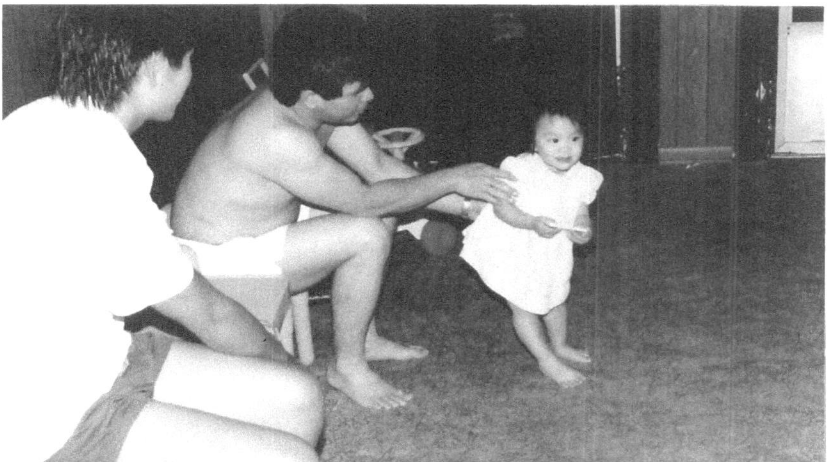

...e in Berne.

Listening to the sermon at church.

David Chiu translating the Englis[h] sermons at church.

They lived a life that had no hope

by June Grove

Second part of a story about Cambodian refugees who escaped Communist rule in their country and, with the help of the people of the Mennonite Church in Berne have been able to find a home in America.

Yin Fong's story of how they escaped is a harrowing one. Since Yin Fong does not speak English, her story was told to me through an interpreter by the name of David Chiu, who is now living in Elkhart, doing evangelistic work, teaching a class at Goshen College, and completing his own education, majoring in computer science.

David Chiu was born and lived in Hong Kong for the first part of his young life. The product of a broken family, he still retained close ties to his mother, brother, and sister, but he had a lot of time to himself while growing up in Hong Kong, and he got mixed up with the wrong crowd. "I robbed, cheated, and lied," he admitted.

In other words, he was a bad character.

But somewhere along the line he became acquainted with some Chinese of one of the Christian churches in Hong Kong. He hadn't ever been religious, but the people of the church treated him so kindly that he began to reassess his life.

The church turned his attitude all around.

David started studying. In fact, that's why he came to America — to advance his training in computer technology. He wants to find a job and send money home to his family — because this is his first commitment.

But after he has fulfilled the obligations to his family — maybe in a couple of years — David plans to go into the ministry.

Since the Taings have been in Berne, David has made the two and a half hour journey from Elkhart to Berne at least every other week — sometimes every week — where he has talked with the refugees, gone to church with them, and through earphones provided by the Mennonite Church, David interprets the sermon to the Taings who attend church every week.

Translating for Yin Fong, David told the story of her family's flight from the Communists of Cambodia.

Yin Fong and her family, along with about 40,000 other Cambodians, decided to make their bid for freedom one dark midnight. They left on foot, not

made arrangements to get them into the United States where they were reunited with their family in Berne. Twenty-seven of them were finally together.

As was mentioned before, none of the group spoke any English when they first got here, but the younger ones are picking it up fast.

Some have jobs and are doing well, thankful for the help of the people of Berne in getting them on their feet.

They have lost the gaunt look, and the fear is gone from their eyes.

They work hard. The kids want a television set, but the parents say that that would detract from their school studies and they need to study hard so they can learn.

They smile a lot now. They seem so eager to make a visitor welcome. Many of them are learning English at sessions

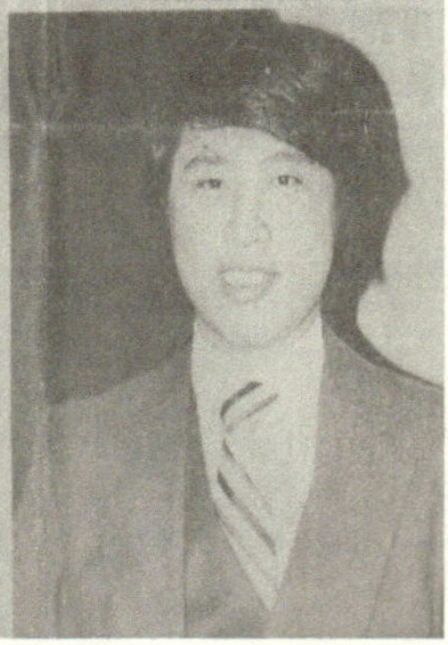

FIRST MENNONITE **update**

October 2, 1979 Vol. 2 No. 21

Welcome To Our New Neighbors

Photo by Mel Liechty

Since late Thursday evening, September 13, when they arrived in Berne, Mr. and Mrs. Taing (pronounced Dang) and their seven children and daughter-in-law have been living in the former Habegger home next to the church.

Mr. Taing, whose first name is Mon Kheang, is 58 years old, and has been a taxi driver and bus driver in Cambodia.

Mrs. Taing, Yin Vuon, is 50 and has been a cottage merchant at home in Battamgang, Cambodia, as well as the mother of nine children.

Ty the oldest son, is 25, his wife, Ky is 20. They have been married about one year.

Sok, the 20-year-old daughter has done some sewing in Cambodia.

Ngou, the second son, is 19, while the two look-alikes Lack and Chhit, also boys, are 14 and 12, respectively.

Poch, the youngest daughter is 10, while Huy is the youngest son at 8 years of age.

Of continuing concern to the family is the welfare of the two daughters, one 28 and the other 22 who are still in Cambodia.

Contrary to what the committee had first been told the older members of the family have all had some schooling. The four smaller children, however, have not been to school because of the unsettled conditions in Cambodia for the past 5 years. It is a fact that no one speaks English as yet, however, all seem very eager and willing to learn and are attending English classes in Fort Wayne.

At a picnic held Sunday, September 23, for the family and all the various committee people most directly involved in their resettlement, Mrs. Taing expressed the family's thanks to the church for their help in bringing them to America.

A very helpful visitor has been David Chiu, student at Mennonite Biblical Seminary in Elkhart. David speaks Chinese and has been coming to Berne with Dr. Howard Charles on Wednesday evenings. He spends the time with the Taing family and has been able to communite with them.

ACKNOWLEDGMENTS

Mom and Dad, there are not enough pages in this book to relay how much you both mean to me. All of the good I have in my life is because of what you overcame and sacrificed throughout my life. Thank you for showing and teaching me what hard work and commitment to family look like. May this book honor you and our family.

To my husband, Brian, for your support and love over the last twenty years. For giving me the beautiful family we have today. I love the life we have built together. You, Grace, and Vivienne mean the world to me.

Engaged Ortho (Vicki Newell, Manon Newell, Sherri Agosta): Thank you for helping, coaching, and working with me to make Warsaw Orthodontics what it is today. We have worked hard together and alongside one another since nearly the very beginning. Vicki, thank you for teaching me how to leverage my strengths and use them effectively to be a great leader. You coached me to communicate effectively and helped me build my confidence one conversation at a time. You helped me learn how powerful my strengths are and that a leadership style is not a one-size-fits-all, but rather something unique and special to each person.

To the First Mennonite Church in Berne, Indiana, and the Mennonite Central Committee for bringing my family to the United States. To Marge Habegger and Maggie Liechty, the two women who were the start and the reason my family made it to the States. I will never forget that it started with you. To the members of the church who formed committees and helped care for my family, taught them English, and provided the support needed to assimilate into life in America. Our deepest gratitude to each of you: Steve and Mary Beth Huser, David Chiu, Fred and Maggie Liechty, Bob and Miriam Liechty, Bill and Linda McKean, Jeanne Stauffer, Gary and Carla Habegger, Barney and Marge Habegger, Ken and Mary Bauman, Iona Amspaugh, Eric Henry, Eldon and Jan Claassen, Millard and Janean Moser, Sherman and Ruth Neuenschwander, Bud and Anita Marble, Jim and Melissa Beitler, Lynn and Doris Liechty, Jeff and Becky Lehman, Kurt and Olga Claussen, Fred Lehman, Donna and Cecil Henn, Fred and Janet Bixler, Larry and Janet Dixon, Wilmer and Kenlyn Sprunger, Jim and Glenna Moser, and John and Mary Eicher.

To my village—my parents, my in-laws, Mary and Dennis Donlan, and our wonderful nanny Lisa Heckaman—thank you for loving and caring for our children with such devotion. Your support has meant the world to me and Brian.

A special thank you to one of my mentors, Dr. O.H. 'Chip' Rigsbee. His wisdom and experience were deeply appreciated during a pivotal time in my practice, and his steady support and generous encouragement have left a lasting impact.

To my team at Warsaw Orthodontics—thank you for placing your trust in me, for your unwavering support, and for the dedication you bring each day to create exceptional experiences for the families we serve. I'm deeply grateful for each of you and the unique talents you contribute to our practice

Finally, to all those who have supported me in ways big and small—whether through encouragement, kindness, or quiet acts of generosity—thank you. If I've inadvertently left anyone out, please accept my sincere apologies. Your presence and support have meant more than I can express, and I carry that gratitude with me always.

ABOUT THE AUTHOR

Dr. Emily Taing Watson is an orthodontist, speaker, and the proud daughter of Cambodian refugees who survived the Khmer Rouge regime. Their story of resilience, strength, and sacrifice lies at the heart of her debut book, *Roots of Resilience*—a tribute to their journey and the enduring life lessons that continue to shape her personal values and professional leadership.

Dr. Watson earned her undergraduate degree from Butler University, her Doctor of Dental Medicine from the Boston University Goldman School of Dental Medicine, and completed her orthodontic residency at the Indiana University School of Dentistry. Guided by empathy, discipline, and purpose, she draws deeply from her family's legacy to lead with integrity in both her practice and her broader community.

She resides in Warsaw, Indiana, with her husband, Brian, and their two daughters, Grace and Vivienne, who inspire her daily and serve as a constant reminder of the power of love and resilience.

www.ingramcontent.com/pod-product-compliance
Lightning Source LLC
LaVergne TN
LVHW050550120926
847757LV00002B/29

* 9 7 9 8 8 9 1 8 8 1 2 5 9 *